Praise for

Get It!

"We 'GET IT' and so should you! A terrific guide for a 'GO-TO GAL'!"

—Kathie Lee Gifford and Hoda Kotb

"As an avid health and wellness advocate myself, I found *Get It!* to be a great guide for all women who want to be the best they can be."

—Joan Lunden, award-winning journalist and bestselling author

Get It!

Get It!

A Beauty, Style, and Wellness Guide to Getting Your "It" Together

Jacqueline Laurita
and Jené Luciani

BenBella Books, Inc.
Dallas, TX

BenBella Books, Inc.
PO Box 572028
Dallas, TX 75357-2028
www.benbellabooks.com
Send feedback to feedback@benbellabooks.com

Printed in the United States of America
10 9 8 7 6 5 4 3 2 1

Library of Congress Cataloging-in-Publication Data
Names: Laurita, Jacqueline, author. | Luciani, Jene, author.
Title: Get it! : a beauty, style, and wellness guide to getting your "It"
    together / Jacqueline Laurita and Jene Luciani.
Description: Dallas, Texas : BenBella Books, Inc., [2016] | Includes
    bibliographical references and index.
Identifiers: LCCN 2015051079 (print) | LCCN 2016007319 (ebook) | ISBN
    9781940363844 (trade cloth : alk. paper) | ISBN 9781940363943 (electronic)
Subjects: LCSH: Beauty, Personal. | Women—Health and hygiene. | Fashion.
Classification: LCC RA778 .L38 2016 (print) | LCC RA778 (ebook) | DDC
    646.7/042—dc23
LC record available at http://lccn.loc.gov/2015051079

Editing by Leah Wilson and Heather Butterfield
Copyediting by Stacia Seaman and Shannon Kelly
Proofreading by Karen Wise and Brittany Dowdle
Text design by Faceout Studios

Text composition by PerfecType, Nashville, TN
Cover by Sarah Dombrowsky
Cover illustration by Ralph Voltz
Printed by Versa Press

Distributed by Perseus Distribution
www.perseusdistribution.com

To place orders through Perseus Distribution:
Tel: (800) 343-4499
Fax: (800) 351-5073
Email: orderentry@perseusbooks.com

Special discounts for bulk sales (minimum of 25 copies) are available.
Please contact Aida Herrera at aida@benbellabooks.com.

To my children, Ashlee, CJ, and Nicholas, who are my greatest blessings in life, and to my rock, my everything, my husband Chris.

—Jacqueline

To GiGi and Kalen: You continuously inspire me to be a better person, mom, and role model.

And to my life-long friend Jacquelyn Mariah Porreca: Rest in peace, girlfriend. This one's for you.

—Jené

CONTENTS

INTRODUCTION

One thing I've learned is that no matter how perfect someone's life may appear from the outside, everyone faces challenges and has their ups and downs. The grass may *look* greener in your neighbor's yard, but start rolling around in it and you'll surely find some hidden rocks and weeds. No matter who we are, there is always at least one area in our lives where we're struggling, whether it's our finances, our health, our relationships, our spirituality, our home, our time management, or our work.

For those of you who have followed me through my journey as one of the original cast members of *The Real Housewives of New Jersey*, you are familiar with some of my own struggles. Over the show's six seasons, I've shared with millions of viewers my miscarriages, relationship struggles, and family issues; my body insecurities and my fears of driving on highways and public speaking; the devastating news of my youngest son's autism diagnosis; and the financial struggles our family has faced. Life has not always been a bed of roses for me, but one thing is certain: I will always pick myself up, and I will always rebuild. I will never give up.

For me, the key to surviving whatever life throws your way is in how you choose to perceive situations and react to them. It's keeping a sense of humor. It's finding balance and purpose. It's realizing your strengths and exploring and focusing on what you're passionate about. It's sharing your knowledge with others in hopes of making someone else's life a little easier, more enjoyable, and more fulfilling. It's allowing yourself quality time to create your own beauty from the inside out. When you take care of your own needs and desires, you will be in a much better position to care for and serve others.

I've been interested in the wellness and beauty industries as far back as I can remember. I have a background in health and fitness; when I attended community college in Arizona, I studied body conditioning, weight training, nutrition, biology, anatomy, and physiology. I have also been a licensed cosmetologist for over twenty years. I've worked in salons doing hair, behind a department store's makeup counter, as a freelance makeup artist, as a convention model, and with various hair, makeup, and skin-care companies.

I've also worked with chemists and formulators to develop new beauty products. I've tested and given advice and reviews on many beauty products for a number of websites and national magazines, as well as for beauty PR and consulting firms.

I've done beauty roundups on national TV and I've been a spokesperson for various doctors and beauty products in order to educate consumers.

I do all this because it brings me joy, and that joy helps me push through life's obstacles. When I take care of myself, I feel better about myself, and I have always enjoyed helping others look and feel beautiful, too. I decided to write this book because I want to share my passion and my years of experience in the beauty industry with you in hopes that it will help you and bring you joy as well. In it, I've included my tips, tricks, and secrets

to finding beauty from the inside out so you can be the best you can be. Together with Jené Luciani— my friend, fashion stylist, bra expert, and author of *The Bra Book*—I'll help you *get centered*, *get on track*, *get organized*, *get healthy*, *get fit*, *get beautiful hair*, *get flawless skin*, *get made up*, and *get stylish and sexy*!

Jené and I believe that taking care of ourselves mentally and physically helps us be our best, so that we can give our best to others. To be constantly improving and evolving, we need to believe in ourselves, no matter the difficulties we face. During those rough patches, learn what you can from the experience and keep the faith. Keep believing that "this too shall pass," because it can only rain for so long; eventually, the sun will come out. With a little luck, a lot of hard work, and a positive attitude, you can have whatever you want out of life; you just have to go *get it*!

—*Jacqueline*

❧

There's one question I seem to get asked all the time: "How do you juggle everything on your plate and still make time for yourself?" That question is usually followed by: "You must be exhausted/superhuman/crazy."

While I can definitely relate to all of those adjectives on any given day, making it all work is something I have to work *at* on a daily basis in order to maintain my sanity and keep my life running smoothly. Although I do sport a Wonder Woman tattoo, I unfortunately don't harness any superhuman powers. I'm fortunate to have a career doing something I love, albeit in a very tough and competitive industry where you have to hustle for every booking and job. My other job title—Mom—I of

course wear proudly, but it only adds to the juggling act I do every day. I know you all can relate!

Many of you know me from my regular fashion, beauty, and lifestyle segments on TV shows like *NBC's Today*, *Wendy Williams*, *Meredith*, *Dr. Oz*, and many others. Becoming a nationally recognized fashion and beauty correspondent was a dream come true, but it didn't happen overnight. It was the result of more than a decade of working behind the scenes in TV production, as well as writing and researching many topics for magazine articles and advice columns. Some of you may also know me as the Bra Lady because I'm the author of the bestseller *The Bra Book*, which came out in 2009 and was just contracted for a second edition!

Writing *The Bra Book* was as personal a decision as it was a professional one; after many years of struggling to find the right bra, something that most every woman struggles with but that was exacerbated for me by a breast deformity, I realized there was a great need for a cohesive and comprehensive resource on that very important topic. Turns out I was right, as women all over the world have embraced *The Bra Book* and its advice, and I'm so grateful!

The same year *The Bra Book* was released, I gave birth to a beautiful daughter named GiGi. At three years old, she was diagnosed with a controversial condition called Sensory Processing Disorder. A lot of the recommendations for managing this condition are similar to those for children on the autism spectrum, so my friend and fellow TV personality Jacqueline Laurita has been a great help and a great resource, having gone through her son Nicholas's autism diagnosis.

In 2014, as I was going through a divorce and Jac and I were just beginning work on this book, I almost lost my life to a massive pulmonary embolism—a blood clot in my lung. This was the result of a genetic predisposition to blood clots that I didn't know I had, coupled with recent birth control pill use, which turned out to be a potentially lethal combination. Rather than letting what happened to me get me down, I wrote about it in *SHAPE* magazine. Afterward, I received many, many letters from women across the country who either have been in similar situations, or told me that my story prompted them to get a blood test before they went on the pill. That's one benefit of living your life like an open book.

My entire career has basically been about using my media presence to help other women, whether by giving them fashion tips to look their best based on their body shape and budget, or by sharing bra-fitting advice. This is truly what I'm passionate about. For me, it's not just about shoes and coats and what's "in" this season. It's also about sharing parts of my life and my own struggles as a busy working mom in an effort to help other women. We all go through trials and tribulations. I believe I've been given a voice, not only as a media personality but also as a writer, so I can use what I've gone through to help others on their journeys.

Writing has always been my passion, and with one successful book under my belt, I've turned my knack for giving useful advice into a lucrative career. When I started thinking about my next book, I realized I wanted to team up with another busy, hard-working gal who also lives a public life but has private struggles too. I'd met Jac through her fitness trainer and our mutual friend Jolene Matthews (who offers her own expertise in this book as well!), and of course I had seen her on *Real Housewives*. I related to the challenges she faced as a wife and mother of a special needs child who was also managing a high-profile career. Her longtime expertise in the beauty industry matched perfectly with my own expertise in health and style. It was clear that Jac was the perfect person to team up with to share some of the things we've learned along the way.

So, we began putting that proverbial pen to paper. Then, less than a year after surviving the pulmonary embolism, surprise! My boyfriend Patrick and I learned that we were expecting a baby boy, whose due date was just a couple of months before this book was set to be released. He and I blended our families, and I'm now living a busy life in upstate New York juggling writing, TV appearances, and family. It's insanely hectic—and I wouldn't have it any other way!

This book isn't just a how-to about beauty, or even about life. It's more of a why-not. Why not figure out ways to carve out time for yourself *without* the guilt? Why not go after your own dreams instead of living someone else's? You're never too busy, too old, or too "stuck" to go out and *get it*, whatever "it" may be for you. Sometimes maybe all "it" is is a much-needed pedicure or five minutes of meditation.

After coming through a divorce and nearly losing my life in the same year, and then, in the following year, making a major move and essentially starting over again, when people ask how I do it, I simply say, "I just do!" Every year, I decide what it is I need to "get" for myself, and then I set those goals. This year? It'll be peace of mind that my children will have the strongest role model they possibly can.

Jac and I hope this book inspires you to make time for yourself and *get* what you need out of life, too!

—Jené

"The highest levels of performance come to people who are centered, intuitive, creative, and reflective—people who know to see a problem as an opportunity."

—Deepak Chopra

CHAPTER 1

Get Centered!

What does it mean to *get centered?* Whether you're a working mom or a single woman trying to climb the career ladder in your chosen field, nothing is more important than finding balance. We've all heard the phrase "it's a juggling act," and let's face it, sometimes we have so many balls in the air, it makes us dizzy trying to keep our focus on them all. Too often, we come close to not only dropping them, but also toppling over ourselves . . . and giving up altogether.

Getting centered means quieting your mind to attain balance and control—and the busier your life is, the more crucial getting centered is to staying sane. Finding a place from which you have control over your thoughts and emotions is a necessary first step to gaining control over the rest of your life. That's why this is the first chapter in this book: it's your foundation and the most important thing you do every day.

We know what you're probably thinking: "I barely have five minutes in the day to go to the bathroom by myself! How am I supposed to find the time to do something *else*?"

Whatever your daily struggles are, trust us, we can relate. We are both busy working moms, each raising multiple children, including one with special needs. You're trying to Keep It All Together, but sometimes the stress can build up to the point where you explode—or implode, and self-destruct. Not a good look for anyone!

When you're feeling stressed and scattered and pulled in a million different directions, and your to-do list is a mile long, *that's* precisely the time to hit the brakes. STOP. Take a deep breath. Find your center.

How do you do that? We certainly don't have all the answers, but we've put together some tips and strategies that have helped us remain centered in our lives—what we've learned not only from our own life experiences, but also from some of the top life coaches and experts in the industry.

Dealing with Strong Emotions

When you are centered, you feel more at peace and self-confident. Your body is relaxed, and your mind is clear to make decisions based on what's best for you and those around you.

Negative emotions like stress and frustration can make a challenging situation worse, preventing you from finding your center and driving you to respond impulsively rather than with intention and control . . . which means you're more likely to say or do things you otherwise would not.

Having good and bad emotions is completely normal, but expressing and acting on them in an acceptable and beneficial way is a skill that can only be mastered through awareness and practice.

Identify Your Emotions

Throughout the day, as you experience feelings and emotions, try to identify and name them. Ask yourself, "Is the emotion I am feeling positive or negative?"

Pay Attention to Who or What Those Negative Emotions Are Associated With

Try to avoid or limit time with those people or things.

Pay Attention to How Your Body Reacts to Those Emotions

Negative feelings can lead to immediate physiological changes like increased heart rate, perspiration,

Put the Oxygen Mask on Yourself before Helping Others

Women, but especially those of us who are mothers, are often expected to be entirely *altruistic*, meaning unselfishly devoted to the welfare of others—so much so that they forget about their own needs and desires as they're dealing with everyone else's. It's easy to lose your center when your partner, kids, other family members, boss, friends, kids' teachers, charity organizations, friends—even your pets—are making demands on your time, each one seeking your full attention. Don't worry; we've all been there. No judgments here. But when life starts to overwhelm you, it's even more important that you make sure your needs are also taken care of. You can't take care of others until you take care of yourself!

dry mouth, shallow breathing, hives, and muscle tension, plus—especially over time—health effects like headaches, stomach cramps, ulcers, and numbness in the face and fingers, just to name a few!

To Calm Your Emotions, Calm Your Body

It's hard to think clearly when your body is having a strong physical response. Fortunately, you can often diminish or even eliminate physical responses once you're aware of them—by carefully focusing on and controlling your breathing or forcing your muscles to relax. Once your body is back under control, it's easier for your mind to follow.

Respond Thoughtfully, Not Emotionally

Ask yourself these questions:

- What am I trying to accomplish in this situation? What do I want the end result to be?

- What are my options for expressing my emotions and what may the consequences be for each option I choose?

"When I'm anxious, it is because I am living in the future. When I am depressed, it is because I am living in the past. We crucify ourselves between two thieves: regret for yesterday and fear of tomorrow."

—Rev. Run

- What are my options for resolving this conflict and what may the consequences be for each option I choose?

- What will happen if I choose not to say or do anything at all?

Consider your options wisely and choose responses that will get you closest to your goals—not the responses that will give you momentary gratification. And if you do decide you want or need to communicate your feelings in the moment, be sure to do so calmly, in a non-threatening way. (Unless, of course, you are on a reality show. In that case, let her rip!)

"This too shall pass."

—King Solomon

Getting Centered When Things Are Out of Your Control

When you are faced with a challenge, it's easy to feel powerless. But the best way to get your head around what you can do—and what you can't—is to ask yourself: *Is this a situation that is out of my control?*

If the answer is no, and there's something you can do to improve the situation, do it! But if the situation legitimately *is* out of your control, making peace with that—and gaining a clearer awareness of what you *can* control—can make a big difference in your emotional response.

- Accept that you are powerless in that situation; trying to control a situation that is out of your control will only add to your anxiety and stress.

- As Elsa sings in *Frozen*: Let it go! Let go of the worry, fear, and stress associated with anticipating the situation's possible outcomes; just deal with each new thing as it happens.

- Accept responsibility for what you could have prevented in the situation and learn what you can from that.

- Choose a more positive perspective of the situation you are in. The one thing that is always in your control is your perception of your situation. You have the power to change that perception and, in the process, your emotional response to any situation at any time.

A Few Ways to Help You *Get Centered*

When you're feeling overwhelmed and need a time-out, here are a few ways to calm down, refresh, and refocus.

Stop and Focus *Only* on Your Breathing

Stop whatever you are doing and thinking immediately and start listening and focusing only on your breath. Slowly take long, deep breaths in through your nose, and then exhale all the way out through your mouth. Do this until you feel your mind and body are calm and controlled.

Disengage and Walk Away

Resist reacting impulsively to negative emotions. Instead, walk away from heated situations until you can calm down, work through them, and respond from a more rational place.

Find and Repeat a Mantra

A mantra is a sound, word, or short phrase that offers you encouragement, inspiration, and motivation; for example, "I am always in control of my words and my actions." Repeating it is designed to help to center your thoughts, reaffirm your goals, and keep you going. Using one can be as simple as mentally repeating the word "breathe" to yourself in stressful situations.

"Meditation is a technique to help us be with ourselves thoroughly and deeply. It allows ourselves the time and space to discover who we are, to discover and face our wild untamed mind and our fears, and to discover the basic goodness of ourselves and our world."

—Jeremy Hayward

Pray and/or Meditate

Find somewhere quiet and focus your thoughts through prayer or meditation like the one described on page 6.

You can also meditate or pray as part of your daily routine—the better you get at clearing, calming, and controlling your mind, the more easily you'll be able to do so during moments of stress. Ten to fifteen minutes is all you need!

Spend Some Time Outside

Getting even a few minutes of sunshine can make a big difference in your state of mind. The vitamin D you get from sunlight increases the levels of a natural antidepressant in your brain called serotonin. And surrounding yourself with nature is a great way to help block out negative thoughts and feelings; clear your mind and awaken your five senses by focusing only on what you see, hear, taste, smell, and touch.

Jacqueline's Daily Meditation

Sit in a position that you find comfortable, but remember your posture, girl; this isn't the time for a nap! Try sitting cross-legged with your back straight, but not rigid, to prevent you from getting sleepy.

Place your right hand in your left hand, palms facing upward, right above your lap and below your belly button. The tips of your thumbs should be slightly raised and lightly touching. Your eyes should be partially open and focused on a peaceful object. (You can close them if you prefer—just don't fall asleep!) Your tongue is gently pressed behind the front teeth. You may choose to light a great-smelling candle or listen to calm, repetitive, and gentle music.

Without letting your mind wander, focus only on the inhale and exhale of your breath. Inhale positivity, blessings, and inspiration and exhale and eliminate the negative thoughts and distractions attacking your mind.

Go for a Power Walk or Do Another Form of Exercise

Exercising relieves stress while it produces mood-boosting endorphins. Try yoga, stretching, boxing, or whatever form of exercise you most enjoy.

Talk to Someone, or Write Down Your Thoughts and Emotions

Venting to an unbiased, trustworthy friend (or a professional!) can help release your negative feelings and let you look at your situation from another perspective. And if no one is available, writing or journaling is another great way to help you process and organize your feelings before reacting to them.

Often, by the time you've finished putting your thoughts into words, you are already on the path to feeling better. After you've released your "inner bitch," your emotions just aren't as intense.

If you're upset with someone in particular and you feel silly just writing in a journal, try the "Write It and Rip It" method: write a letter to the person you're upset with—then, once you're finished writing, rip it up. It's very liberating: write it and let it go!

Stay Positive!

Once you have quieted your mind, the next step to not just getting centered but *staying* centered is to replace negative thoughts with positive ones.

Nothing can knock you off center faster than negative thoughts. The mind is an extremely powerful thing; we can actually turn a negative thought into reality simply by thinking it. Fortunately, the opposite is also true: training ourselves to think positively will help to manifest positive outcomes in our lives.

That doesn't mean things will always go the way we want them to. But keeping a positive attitude, and the positive energy you create in the process, will make your journey in life a better one.

Choose Positive Thoughts

Observe your thoughts throughout the day. Are you choosing positive thoughts—like "I can do this!"—or negative ones—like "What's the point of doing this? I'm really not seeing results I want anyway."

Stop focusing on the negative circumstances in your life and start focusing on all the positive ones. Instead of thinking about the things you *don't* want in your life, think *only* about the things you *do* want!

Choose Positive Perceptions

The way you perceive any situation or circumstance is a choice. When a traffic jam happens on your way to work, do you use your time wisely and productively (listening to audiobooks, returning phone calls, studying notes, or finding peace in the moment) or become anxious and impatient,

lose control, and get angry? You may not be able to change your circumstances, but the way you view them affects how you feel about them and determines the way you respond to them.

Use Positive Affirmations

Positive affirmations are encouraging messages designed to counteract negative thinking. You read or recite them throughout your day, or at certain times each day, until you believe them.

Some of our favorites:

- ▣ I am worthy of love, joy, and success.
- ▣ I am smart and make wise choices.
- ▣ I can find a solution to any problem.
- ▣ I am capable of achieving my goals.
- ▣ I have all the energy I need to do everything I want to do.
- ▣ I am attracting all the right people into my life.

Surround Yourself with Positive People Who Support and Encourage You

The people with whom you surround yourself should be people you love and trust and who love and trust you—people who believe in you, who bring out the best in you, and who will reinforce your positive thoughts and help you triumph over negative ones.

Avoid or limit your time with people who don't have your best interests in mind—or, even if they do, always bring you down or make you doubt yourself. Do not allow their negative thinking to enter your flow of positive thoughts!

Believe in Yourself

As important as it is to deal with your emotions and think positively, all the meditation and mantras in the world won't make a difference in getting and staying centered if you don't believe in yourself and your abilities.

Stop comparing yourself to other people—you have your own unique strengths, talents, and skills. And stop viewing yourself as inferior. Don't obsess with living up to someone else's standards; live in a way that's authentic to who *you* are. Stay true to yourself and be proud of who you are!

Need some help with all of that? We do too sometimes. Here are six things we try to remember to do whenever we feel that belief faltering.

Believe in Your Talents and Skills

Make a list of all the things you are good at. These should be the things that come easy to you and that you feel confident doing. Everybody has skills and challenges and everyone has successes and failures.

Believe in What You Are Trying to Achieve

Ignore others' criticism and doubt in your beliefs and in what you are trying to achieve. It's important for you to believe in what you are doing, even if nobody else does.

Believe Anything Is Possible If You Persevere

No one ever achieved anything by giving up. Always keep trying!

Believe You Deserve What You Want

Everybody deserves to be happy. Everybody is worthy of love, joy, and success.

Believe and Trust That There Is a Higher Power Working Strategically for the Greater Good

We love the message in the lyrics of the song "Unanswered Prayers" by country singer Garth Brooks: "Some of God's greatest gifts are unanswered prayers." Sometimes we want something badly and are convinced it is the best thing for us, then become disappointed when we don't get it—but only because we can't see what is there waiting for us in the future. Sometimes, what we *don't* get makes way for something even greater in our life.

"Believe in yourself and all that you are. Know that there is something inside you that is greater than any obstacle."
—Christian D. Larson

Believe You Are Capable

You must have faith in your abilities to accomplish your goals. Have the self-confidence that you have what it takes to *get it* or that you are capable of learning what it is you need to know in order to *get it*. Nothing and nobody can stop you but yourself! You *can* do it. You *are* capable.

"When you doubt your power, you give power to your doubt."

—Honoré de Balzac

"Three Simple Rules in Life

1. If you do not go after what you want, you'll never have it.

2. If you do not ask, the answer will always be no.

3. If you do not step forward, you will always be in the same place."

—Carey Lohrenz

"To accomplish great things, we must not only act, but also dream; not only plan, but also believe."

—Anatole France

CHAPTER 2

Get on Track!

Now that you've gotten centered in the present, it's time to get on track for your future! When you are on track—meaning, when you have a vision and are steadily working toward achieving your goals—everything you do will start to fall in line. When you're on track, you are focused and productive and live life with purpose, which leads you to feel more fulfilled and happier with your circumstances.

Getting on track starts with knowing exactly what you want each key area of your life to look like. This chapter will help you enliven your soul and achieve and maintain success in all areas of your life through three deceptively simple-sounding steps: discovering your passion, creating a clear vision, and staying motivated.

Discovering Your Passion

Discovering and pursuing your passion is key to finding a sense of fulfillment and joy in your life. What inspires you? If you could do anything you wanted—anything in the world—what would you do?

Sometimes, the best place to start looking for your passion is in your own story. Jené's lifelong struggle with a breast deformity led to writing *The Bra Book* to help other women. After having a child with autism, Jacqueline used her TV platform to advocate for autism awareness, and both of us

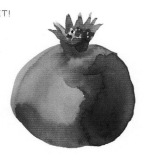

"At the center of your being you have the answer; you know who you are and you know what you want."

—Lao Tzu

have a passion for using our expertise to help other women, which led to writing this book!

To help you discover your passion, we've provided a set of questions below for you to explore. Do your very best to avoid restrictions and judgments—*do not* allow financial considerations, fear of failing, current schedule restrictions, or what others will think of your choices to affect or determine your answers.

You may find you have more than one thing you are passionate about. Fantastic! Maybe you can figure out a way to combine them to create something unique.

As a Child, What Did You Want to Be When You Grew Up?

Even though we grow and evolve as we age, our core interests often remain the same; your childhood interests might provide clues to your current passions, or passions you've forgotten. Try to remember back to your childhood, and think back to what you spent most of your time dreaming about.

Even if your childhood obsession was dressing up Barbie, it doesn't mean you have to choose being a fashion stylist as a career . . . although you may. Jené grew up in her parents' clothing boutique helping her mom with the buying and playing dress up in the dressing rooms! She turned that childhood passion into a career in fashion journalism.

If, like Jené, clothes and fashion are a passion of yours, there are many avenues you can choose to take, even in your spare time, to indulge in your passion and feed your soul. Maybe start a fashion blog, or help others as a personal shopper; volunteer somewhere you can use your skills, or even just make a Pinterest board with all of your favorite styles.

What Are You Good At?

We're all born good at something (and often, many things!). Think about your specific talents—and ask around if you're drawing a blank. Your parents might remember something you showed a special talent for as a child; your best friend may see something in you that you don't.

Maybe you are naturally artistic and love doodling, and would enjoy taking an art class, selling your art, working for an ad agency, or doing interior design. Or maybe you are an amazing organizer and could share your skill and passion for organizing with others on social media, link up with organizational products to help them sell their items, or start a website teaching others. Are you the friend everyone goes to for advice? Consider starting an advice column or podcast, writing a book, or volunteering to speak at a conference.

What Brings You Joy?

What are you the happiest doing? What excites you? What do you love so much that you'd do it for free?

Once you discover what brings you joy, do it! Think about how you can cultivate your passion to make it a greater part of your life—or even turn it into a career. Is being a mom what you love most, and do you wish you could share that love with others? Maybe you can start a mommy group where you facilitate activities and offer support for other moms in your area.

What Have You Always Wanted to Do, but Could Never Find the Time For?

Have you ever said to yourself or others, "I wish I had time to . . ."? That is precisely the thing you need to make time for! Whatever you're craving, it's calling to you, so answer it, feed your soul with it.

"Aim for a star, and keep your sights high! With a heart full of faith within, your feet on the ground, and your eyes in the sky."

—Helen Lowrie Marshall

Creating a Clear Vision

Once you've discovered your passion, the next step to fulfillment and joy is to visualize a life where that passion is a part of it. Maybe your passion is something you want to share with the world. Maybe you want to live your passion quietly at home. Either of these is okay! But to reach the future you want, you first need to have a clear vision of it.

If you can't see in your mind's eye what you wish for your life, it's impossible to formulate a plan to make that vision a reality.

Break down in detail what you want your life to look like. What do you spend your time doing? What organizations or online communities are you a part of? What is your job or career? Is your body healthy, strong, flexible, and fit? What does your diet consist of? What's your style? Are you organized and productive? Are you great with time management? Are you in a loving, reciprocal relationship? Describe the details of your perfect partner. Where are you living? What does your house look like? What style of

How to Create a Vision Board

1. **Buy a poster board or corkboard.**

2. **Create a theme.** Your theme can be general—your vision for your future, or what your ideal life would look like—or a specific goal. Choose a theme that inspires you.

3. **Find and collect pictures that depict your vision.** You can get these from magazines, newspapers, or the internet, or you can even draw your own. Make sure the images symbolize experiences you want to have or people, places, and things that you want in your life.

4. **Arrange your pictures visually.** If you're doing one big vision board, you may want to group certain images into sections—for example, one section might focus on relationships and home life, another on jobs and career.

5. **Attach the pictures to your poster board.** Use glue if you're using poster board, or tacks if using a corkboard.

6. **Add positive affirmations, motivational sayings, and/or quotes.**

7. **Get creative!** You can use paint or markers or attach ribbon or fabrics, scrapbook-style. You can even place a happy picture of yourself in the center of the board. Do whatever speaks to you! It's your vision!

Not very crafty? You can always create an e-vision board instead, either using something like Pinterest or simply by opening up a Word document on your computer or a "note" on your smartphone, and listing your specific, vision-related goals!

furniture do you own? What kind of car are you driving? How many kids do you have? Do you have any pets? If so, what kind? What achievements do you see yourself making?

There are lots of different ways to make sure you're creating a clear vision. We read a story recently about a man who, every time he had a specific goal, changed his computer password to a specific short phrase that reminded him of that goal every time he logged in. He used this technique to improve his relationship, and even to quit smoking. It's amazing what the power of having a vision can do to manifest it in reality!

One of our favorite ways to help visualize what you want from life—and keep that vision front and center—is to create a vision board. (We've included instructions here for you to make your own!) You can make one vision board for all of your visualizations, or you can create separate boards for different goals or different key areas of your life.

Once you're finished, put your vision board in a place where you can view it easily and often. Look at your vision board for at least one to five minutes daily! It's best to see it first thing in the morning and last thing before you go to bed.

Do vision boards work? We certainly think so! Jené dreamed of meeting Oprah and showing her *The Bra Book* because Oprah's numerous shows about helping women look and feel better with the right bra inspired Jené to write the book in the first place, so her vision board above her desk contained pictures of Oprah. One day, she was invited to an event Oprah would be attending. She showed up, book in hand, as many others did, hoping to get five minutes to chat with the talk-show queen. No one else was able to get near her. Just as Oprah was about to walk onstage, Jené hid behind a pole (true story!) and quickly grabbed the chance to show Oprah her book. Oprah said that she was glad Jené chose to tackle this topic because it was "very important for women." The next day, her publicist received a call from Oprah's producers saying that Jené must have made an impression on her. Although Oprah's famous talk show ended shortly thereafter, Jené felt she fulfilled her goal of getting an "endorsement" from the TV queen. When opportunity meets drive and determination, there's no telling what you can do!

Staying Motivated

Motivation is the force that drives us to work toward the things we desire. It is what pushes us into finally taking action in pursuing our goals. It is our incentive, our inspiration, and the fuel behind our success.

"What you do today will determine where you are tomorrow. Are you moving forward or standing still?"

—Tom Hopkins

The most effective kind of motivation is internal motivation: dissatisfaction with your current situation and the desire to make your life better. If you've identified your passion and clarified your vision of your future, you're already halfway there! Once you know what you want your life to look like, you can start working toward it.

So it's just that easy? Well, no. Not usually. But the main reason why achieving our goals can be so difficult is that we tend to get in our own way, sabotaging our efforts to change.

What Is Stopping Me from Staying Motivated and Pursuing the Success and Happiness I Desire?

If this is an issue for you (and it can be for all of us, sometimes), you may already know what it is that is preventing you from going after what you want—but you may not. Here are a few common things that may be holding you back, and some help on getting past them.

YOU LACK CONFIDENCE IN YOURSELF OR YOUR ABILITIES, OR THINK YOU'RE UNDESERVING

Everyone deserves to be happy and successful, and we all have valuable skills and talents. You must have faith and believe in yourself, even if nobody else will. However, we know that sometimes, that's easier said than done!

The good news is that just saying it makes a big difference. Whenever you find yourself thinking that you can't do something or don't deserve to have something, erase that negative self-talk by replacing it with positive affirmations like "I can do this" or "I've got this!"

"One important key to success is self-confidence. An important key to self-confidence is preparation."

—Arthur Ashe

Positive self-talk takes practice, but used regularly, it has the power to boost your confidence as well as your chances of achieving the success you *are* capable of having and *do* deserve.

And if you don't yet have the precise skills you need to go after what you want? There isn't much that is beyond your capability to learn. So get to it. Learn what you lack!

YOU FEAR FAILURE

It feels safer to give up than to attempt a challenge. But by not trying, you are, by default, preventing yourself from reaching your goals.

The only way to get past this fear is to push through it. Try starting with smaller lower-stakes goals to help build your confidence. Whether you succeed or not, facing your fears and overcoming them—and seeing that even if you *do* fail, the attempt was still worthwhile—will leave you feeling braver and more empowered to face larger challenges.

Sometimes the best way to get past a fear of failing is to think through the actual consequences of failing—and of failing to try! Frequently, what happens if you *do* fail isn't as scary as it first seemed. Ask yourself:

◙ What do I imagine would happen if I failed? And then what? And then what? Why do those things scare me?

◙ How would I feel if I never attempted to reach my goal? Would I have any regrets? Would I be disappointed in myself?

You can change your perception of failing by viewing failure as part of the process of learning. Think of failure as an opportunity to grow and evolve as an individual.

YOU FEAR SUCCESS

To some of you, a fear of success may sound silly. Maybe you're thinking, "Who wouldn't want to succeed?" But you'd be surprised at how common it is. Many people are afraid of what happens if they achieve success. They're afraid they will somehow screw it up and won't be able to maintain it. They're afraid they may disappoint others or themselves, or that others in their life will respond to their success negatively.

Just as in the previous section, ask yourself:

"It is hard to fail, but it is worse never to have tried to succeed."
—Theodore Roosevelt

◙ What do I imagine would happen if I succeeded? And then what? Why do those things scare me?

Replace these negative fears with positive thinking; list all of the reasons things can and will work out the way you want them to. Achieving success takes a lot of planning, hard work, effort, perseverance, and sacrifice, and you deserve to feel good about your accomplishments, not be afraid of them!

YOU LISTEN TO THE NEGATIVITY, DOUBTS, AND OPINIONS OF OTHERS

While other people can often provide you with valuable advice and perspective, believing in others' opinions over your own—especially when those opinions are negative—can leave you discouraged.

"You'll always miss 100 percent of the shots you don't take."
—Wayne Gretzky

Avoid or limit your time with people who bring you down or derail you from accomplishing your goals. It doesn't matter what anyone else believes about you or your ideas; it matters how *you* feel about yourself and what you are trying to achieve.

YOU FEEL SAFER PUTTING OTHERS' NEEDS BEFORE YOUR OWN

Women in general tend to be trained from birth to be caring and nurturing to those around us, usually to the detriment of our own needs. Because of this, it often feels safer to fall back on this role than to work toward things you want for yourself.

Stop attending to others' needs as an excuse to neglect your own. Learn when say "no" to the other people in your life and start saying "yes" more often to yourself!

YOU ARE EASILY DISCOURAGED BY A MISTAKE OR SETBACK, OR WHEN YOU ARE NOT SEEING THE RESULTS YOU WANT FAST ENOUGH

Sometimes things just don't come easy. You need to accept that you will need to put in the work to get what you want . . . and just go for it. Take it day by day, and keep the momentum going forward. Keep reminding yourself that you are *one* day closer to your goal than if you had chosen to do nothing at all.

"Never leave that till tomorrow which you can do today."
—Benjamin Franklin

Even when you make a mistake, it does not mean that you will never be good or successful at what you are trying to do. Try to view your mistakes as opportunities to grow and learn. Dissect what went wrong. If needed, take responsibility for your mistakes; don't blame others or make excuses, or you will only repeat the same mistakes in the future. Instead, ask yourself what you could have done better, then regroup and take action to do things differently going forward.

How to Fight Procrastination

Procrastination, whatever the cause, is usually the main thing keeping us from achieving our goals. To leave procrastinating in the dust, stop making excuses as to why you can't get things done and start focusing on all the reasons that you must make them happen! Stop thinking about why you *can't* do something and start figuring out ways you *can*. Be proactive and start NOW!

Other ways to help overcome procrastination:

- Break down tasks into smaller pieces that are easier and quicker to achieve.
- Put a time frame on what needs to be done. Give yourself a deadline!
- Focus on the positive rewards of accomplishing your goals.

Some Ways to Stay Motivated

Even with all those obstacles out of the way, sustaining motivation can be hard! Here are a few tips for maintaining your drive over the long term:

- Use a system of rewards and consequences to keep yourself focused.

- Research inspirational success stories of people who have been where you are and/or have accomplished something you are striving for.

- Seek out mentors who inspire you and model the qualities, skills, capabilities, and expertise that you desire.

- Surround yourself with positive people who support and encourage you.

- Remind yourself of the resources you can draw on to help you achieve your goals—whether that's your own skills or the advice of others.

- Read or listen to self-improvement books/audiobooks or inspirational/motivational CDs or DVDs.

- Track your progress. Checking things off of your list as you complete them gives you a sense of accomplishment and makes you feel great! Nothing's more motivating than seeing how far you've already come.

"Many of life's failures are people who did not realize how close they were to success when they gave up."

—Thomas A. Edison

"Organization isn't about perfection; it's about efficiency, reducing stress and clutter, saving time and money, and improving your overall quality of life."

—Christina Scalise

CHAPTER 3

Get Organized!

I f you are a busy woman who wears many hats throughout the day (the mom hat, the wife hat, the friend hat, the chef hat, the chauffeur hat, the worker hat, the nurse hat—you get the idea!), you know how quickly life can become overwhelming. You're bombarded with nagging thoughts and constant reminders of things you've yet to accomplish, and endless demands waiting impatiently to be addressed.

There are days when there don't seem to be enough hours to get everything done that you need to get done. And when you feel overburdened, you may shut down. When you shut down, you don't complete your daily tasks and you can end up feeling even more overwhelmed, inadequate, and discouraged. An unfinished workload can feel like a never-ending uphill battle. And if you're always playing catch-up, it's impossible to move ahead.

That's why it's so important to *get organized*—in your thoughts and in your environment. It's the key to becoming more productive and more effective, in all areas of your life. Getting organized

means having the peace of mind that your life is under your control. It means knowing when you can fit in a workout and where you put that bok choy you bought for dinner. It means it will be easier and faster to find that outfit you wanted to wear and the right makeup tools. Organization is essential to really *get* what you want and need out of life, whatever that might be.

We know it's not an easy task—but it *is* well worth the effort!

D.R.O.P. Everything and Refocus!

It's hard to clearly focus on one task when you are fixated on and stressed about others. Sometimes there are just too many thoughts going on inside your head about what you need to do for you to focus on any one thing, making it impossible to actually get things done.

There's a tool we like to use when this happens to us to help us think and work more effectively: we

D.R.O.P. everything—download, rearrange, organize, and proceed—and refocus!

Download

When you start feeling overwhelmed by your thoughts, *stop* and physically "download" them, whether on paper (a pocket-size notebook works well for this) or digitally (into a smartphone app or text document). Get them *out* of your mind, before you *lose* your mind! Physically being able to see your thoughts lets you process them more effectively.

Rearrange

Once you have your thoughts on paper (or screen), rearrange them into categories: home, work, family, and personal, for example. Then use this to turn those thoughts into specific tasks, projects, and goals.

Let's say that under the home category, you've added—based on your download—things like "clean closet," "clean out pantry," and "buy groceries." Under each of these, write a step-by-step

On Jené and Jacqueline's Smartphones

We use apps like OmniFocus, a task management platform for Mac, iPad, or iPhone, and Evernote, a digital workspace productivity app where you can write, collect, discuss, and present your ideas, to keep each key area of our lives in order. We also use Fantastical 2, a calendar app for OS X, to manage and organize our calendars, events, and reminders.

list of how you will accomplish the task. For example, under "clean closet," your list might look like this: (1) Separate clothes into keep, give away/donate, trash, alter, dry-clean, and wash piles. (2) Put keep pile back in the closet. (3) Wash clothes. And so on.

"Get Organized and you'll have Order. Have Order and you'll maintain Control. Stay in Control and you'll have unlocked Freedom."

Organize

After you've placed your thoughts in category sections, organize them in order of priority. Then move those items, in priority order, onto a to-do list and add a time frame or deadline for each task or project, where applicable. You want to be able to look at this list throughout the day to remind yourself to stay on task. You can even send reminder alarms to your phone for the most urgent action items, so they stay on your mind until you can cross them off your list.

Proceed

Review your to-do list daily and take action! Here are some tips for knocking out items on your list as efficiently as possible:

- Don't procrastinate. If a task can be done in five minutes or less, do it immediately!

- Do what you can get done based on where you are. What can you do while on the road? At home? At work? Lying in bed? Waiting in line somewhere?

- Break bigger tasks into smaller increments that allow you to make progress on them daily.

Finding the Time

We used to constantly find ourselves saying "I don't have time to _____," but when we really thought about it, we realized that we actually *did* have pockets of time throughout our day we could use to do more things. We just weren't choosing to use that time wisely.

The issue is almost never that we don't have the time, but that we don't choose to *make* the time. It's so easy to get distracted! If you block time on your calendar, time becomes available.

- Take notice of when during the day you have peak energy and low energy, and organize your day accordingly. Schedule tasks that don't require as much brainpower for lower-energy periods.

Organizing Your Home

No matter how organized your to-do list is, it's hard to get anything done when the space around you is in chaos.

Here are our tips for creating a beautiful, peaceful, organized living space—quickly and simply!

"Have nothing in your house that you do not know to be useful, or believe to be beautiful."

—William Morris

Declutter Your Space

Decluttering your mind starts with decluttering your environment. Clutter makes your home not only harder to organize, but also harder to keep tidy.

To get started decluttering, follow these tips:

▣ Work on just one room—or one section of a room—at a time to keep the process from feeling too overwhelming.

▣ Break the room or room section down further into smaller ten-minute projects to tackle during minibreaks during your day.

▣ For decluttering that needs to be done regularly, assign those projects a day of the week—for example, clean out the fruit drawer of the fridge every Monday.

When evaluating items while decluttering:

▣ For each item, decide whether to trash it, recycle it, fix it, donate it, save it, or sell it.

▣ If you haven't used it in a long time, don't use it frequently, don't like it anymore, or don't need it—get rid of it!

▣ When in doubt, throw it out!

Find a Place for Everything

Once you've busted all of the clutter in your home, it's time to get things organized!

▣ Make sure everything has a place, designating certain rooms or drawers or storage bins for certain objects. It makes it much easier to

10-Minute Decluttering Project Ideas

Clean under a sink.

Clean out a junk drawer.

Get rid of all single socks or socks with holes.

Clean off one shelf in the pantry, checking for expired items to toss.

Clean off one shelf in the refrigerator.

Go through one section of your closet looking to throw away, give away, or donate.

Gather and start a single load of laundry.

Wash or put away dishes.

Throw away old, expired, or unwanted toiletries and makeup.

Make the beds.

Gather all your knickknacks on a table and get rid of what you don't want anymore.

Check for any kids' toys you can throw away, give away, or donate.

put things away when you've already decided where they go!

▣ Label, label, label. Label storage bins and other containers. Label cords and chargers with what they belong to. Labeling things will help you find what you need, when you need it, more easily.

- ▣ Get creative! Find new purposes for old or throwaway items, such as rolling up panty hose into cardboard toilet paper rolls and labeling with a Sharpie. (As a bonus, this also keeps panty hose from snagging in drawers!)

TIPS FOR TACKLING A FEW COMMON TROUBLE SPOTS

Warranty Booklets, Appliance Manuals, and Service Receipts

- ▣ Buy a file box and file folders.

- ▣ Group manuals into file folders by room or other category (kitchen appliances, toys, warranties, service records from household maintenance, etc.).

- ▣ Label and alphabetize.

- ▣ Periodically, perhaps once a year, review the box contents and throw away any warranties that have expired and manuals for appliances you no longer have.

Kitchen Pantry

After taking everything out and wiping down shelves and surfaces:

- ▣ Check expiration dates and throw away expired food items.

- ▣ Group like items together. Put beans with other beans in a canned vegetable section; put pasta with other pasta, cereals with other cereals, snacks with other snacks, etc.

- ▣ Buy containers for bulk items (cereal, pasta, nuts, seeds, etc.) and label them. Transfer foods from original packaging into the new bulk containers.

- ▣ Buy can stackers for canned food items.

- ▣ Keep labels—of bulk containers or canned foods—facing forward so you can find everything quickly and easily.

Holiday and Gift-Wrap Storage

- ▣ Buy big bins and label each one by holiday. Fill the bin with its corresponding holiday items. Be sure to also label the specific contents in each bin (holiday stuffed animals, Christmas lights, Christmas ornaments, Halloween costumes, Easter baskets and plastic eggs, winter clothes, etc.).

▢ Buy a wrapping-paper bin. Along with wrapping paper, it can hold scissors, tape, and gift labels and tags for easy access come present-wrapping time.

CREATE HOUSEHOLD KITS

Create household kits to group together related items. Keep the kits in labeled stackable plastic bins, decorated cardboard boxes, or shoeboxes. Get creative! Besides the obvious sewing and first-aid kits, here are just a few ideas of kit types and what they might contain:

▢ Manicure/pedicure kit: supplies needed for manis/pedis, such as foot soak, foot scrub, lotion, cuticle oil, callus remover, cuticle pusher, nail file, nail clippers, baby power, foot spray, etc.

▢ Cords and chargers kit: labeled cords and chargers to phones, computers, cameras, etc.

▢ Bill-pay kit: envelopes, stamps, pens, checkbook, list of monthly bills and debt, etc. You can even put each item in a file folder and put these in a filing box with your bills.

▢ Eyebrow grooming kit: eyebrow brushes, stencils, pencils, powder, gel, tweezers, baby tooth-numbing gel, small scissors, waxing kit, etc.

▢ Tooth fairy kit: tooth holder, labeled baby teeth in baggies, tooth fairy diary, etc.

▢ Thank-you card kit: thank-you notes, envelopes, mailing and/or decorative stamps, stickers, etc.

Create an Order for Quick Cleaning

Once everything in your house is organized, cleaning should be much easier because everything now has a place. If you're still overwhelmed with where to start, however, try these steps for a quick tidy that makes a big difference!

1. Throw away all the trash you can find in your house.

2. Collect dirty laundry, sort it, and start a load.

3. Collect and clean dirty dishes, pots, and pans.

4. Make the bed or beds.

5. Put loose shoes back in their appropriate place.

6. For households with kids: Put toys in their toy bins.

7. Clean up counters and other surfaces where mail and extraneous papers seem to collect.

8. Notice what still needs cleaning, and add that to your to-do list for later!

Make a Chore Jar

Making a chore jar is fun for everyone in your household. It gives you a specific task to do, which eliminates the feeling of being over-whelmed by where to start. You pick it, you do it!

Make your own house rules on how many chores must be picked from the jar each day—but a reward system is also always a good idea. For your kids, try a small, set amount of money or some other concrete reward, like getting to do a preferred activity. For yourself, try a sweet treat or a facial. Everyone loves positive rein-forcement!

Here's how to do it:

- Make a list of the rooms in your house and tasks associated with each room.
- Create slips of paper labeled with one of the rooms in your house on one side and a chore associated with that room on the back.
- Fold the paper slips with the chore on the inside and put them into a jar.
- Have everyone in your household—including yourself—pick slips of paper from the jar and complete the tasks!

"You Gotta Know When to Fold 'Em"

You can take on the task of closet cleaning all at once if you have the time and are feeling inspired one day, or you can break this process down by working one section at a time, a little every day, until it is completed. You decide. There is no need to feel overwhelmed! Here's a step-by-step list to guide you through the process:

- Take everything out of your closet (or out of a section you can handle).
- Wipe everything down, including the hangers, because they get dusty too. Baby wipes work pretty well!

- Make five neat piles of clothes you will keep, give away/donate, throw away, dry-clean, alter, or wash.

- Put all of the keep items back into your closet (see the following tips on closet organization), and then deal with the remaining piles accordingly.

Here are some questions to ask yourself as you are cleaning out your closet and deciding whether or not to keep pieces of clothing.

- Do I have something similar? Which is better? (And which should I get rid of?)

- Do I have anywhere to wear this?

- Have I worn this in the last two years?

- Does this still fit?

- Is this still in style?

- Does this have holes or tears that aren't worth repairing?

- Is this right for my body type? (More on this in chapter 9.)

And remember: When in doubt, get it out!

Our Rules for Closet Organization

- No wire hangers allowed! We all have them, but they don't retain the shape of your clothes very well. The thin velvet-covered ones are the best, especially for fragile materials like silk—and for saving space in your closet!

- All hangers and clothes should face the same direction for easy access.

- Clothes should be grouped by color from dark to light (with the darkest colors at the bottom of a stack).

- Tops should be hung in groups by sleeve length, from longest sleeves to shortest sleeves, so it's quick and easy to take stock of what you have.

- Fold sweaters, sweatshirts, sweatpants, jeans, leggings, T-shirts, and cotton tank tops.

- Hang dresses, skirts, blouses, jackets, and zip-up hoodies.

- Put jeans in stacks by color and style or brand, from darkest to lightest (with darkest on the bottom of the pile)—again, so it's easy to take stock.

- Separate undergarments (bras, underwear, fitted undergarments, panty hose and tights, socks) into drawers, baskets, or bins and group by color and style.

Clever Closet Storage Solutions

- Hang flip-flops on skirt and pants hangers for easy access.

- Store and display clutches in letter organizers.

- Store bikini separates in bins in labeled zip-top bags. (You'll never have to search for the matching bottoms again!)

- Clip dollar-store plastic ring shower hooks on a hanger to store and display tank tops, scarves, or handbags, and use metal shower hooks to hang jeans (they stay wrinkle free, plus you can see what you have more easily!). Or simply put the metal hook right on the closet bar and hang your jeans by the belt loops.

- Use old foam pool noodles or seltzer bottles to put into boots on the closet floor to help them retain their shape.

Jewelry Storage Solutions

Although a jewelry box is the most obvious place for your jewelry, there are also more creative storage solutions. Here are some ideas, broken down by jewelry type.

"Organizing is what you do before you do something, so that when you do it, it is not all mixed up."

—A. A. Milne

- Earrings can be kept in egg trays, ice-cube trays, a tackle box, a weekly pill divider box, hanging on a dream catcher, or on a piece of screen with the edges framed.

- Bracelets can be kept in a basket, divided or color coordinated in sheer bags, on a paper towel holder, or in an underwear divider in a drawer.

- Necklaces can be kept tacked on a corkboard or screen divider, or hanging on a hanger in your closet.

- Rings can be kept in egg trays, ice-cube trays, pencil baskets, or on a fake hand.

Setting Up Your Own Organized, Dedicated Workspace

Having a dedicated and organized home office can dramatically increase your productivity and ability to meet your goals, whether you're running a company or just making sure your bills get paid. Here's our plan for putting together a home office space that works for you!

Stock Up on Supplies

To get your workspace or home office organized, you may need to stock up on some supplies first. Here's our list of organizational items to consider purchasing:

- corkboard and/or magnetic board, plus tacks or magnets

- wall calendar

- filing cabinet or filing container, plus hanging file folders

- flat open trays ("inbox," "outbox," "sort later")

- labeling tool

- binders and dividers

- small and large jars

Organize Your Office

Once you have your office supplies, it's time to get your office organized!

- Keep binders with labeled dividers or use filing boxes, drawers, or cabinets to organize loose papers and other important documents.

- Group your pencils, pens, markers, highlighters, etc., together in one or multiple jars.

- Put small items like magnets, paper clips, rubber bands, staples, tacks, etc., in containers, like spice or baby food jars to keep them separate and organized.

- Use a corkboard above your desk to pin up ideas written on sticky notes or small slips of paper, for brainstorming thoughts or reminders, and to hang your calendar, so it's somewhere you can always see it.

Organize Your Emails

In an office space, getting digital clutter under control is just as important as eliminating physical clutter.

Here's how you can take charge of your email—business or personal:

- Create categories of folders. These should include both action folders—like Immediate Response Required and Opportunities—and archive folders—Personal, School, Work, etc.

- At least once a day, go through your inbox and classify each email: respond, print/scan, delete, or file. (You may need one day to go through all of your past emails to catch up before you can regularly start to maintain it.)

- If a response is needed, put the email into the appropriate action folder. (Make sure you return to this folder after sorting through the rest of your new emails!)

- If the email is something you need to print for future reference, print it right then, and file as needed.

- Delete emails where action is no longer required.

- If you need or want to keep a digital copy, file it in the right archive folder.

"Don't agonize, organize."

—Florynce Kennedy

"To keep the body in good health is a duty, otherwise we shall not be able to keep our mind strong and clear."

—Buddha

CHAPTER 4

Get Healthy!

You're busy, you're tired, and the last thing you want to do is cook a big extensive dinner. We've all been there. Sometimes it seems like that fast-food drive-through is the only option—it's either that or risk not eating at all. Before you know it, after too many of these trips, the scale is creeping up, your energy level is low, and you're feeling sluggish. And what you are putting into your mouth could be to blame.

In this chapter, we're here to help you stop those fast-food trips and other bad eating habits in order to get you healthy. We aren't nutritionists—we are just busy moms who know that the more energy we have, the better we can keep up with our kids, careers, or whatever else life entails! We have also read through enough diet and health books to see a common thread, and we've tried and tested enough healthy diets to know what has worked best for the both of us. What we have learned is that healthy eating is a lifestyle and a choice. And it is actually very simple once you get the hang of it!

How to Eat Better (in 5 Simple Steps)

Eating healthy doesn't have to be a huge challenge. It simply means providing the body with the right nutrients to function at an optimal level, in order to maintain or improve your overall health and longevity. We've provided some simple steps below to help you eat better, and ultimately feel better.

1. Control Your Portions and Fill Half Your Plate with Veggies

It's no secret that food portion sizes have increased over the years, and unfortunately, so has the percentage of Americans who are overweight. Let's get back to the basics! As a general rule, portion sizes should be the size of your fist or fit into your cupped hand. (That equates to about one cup, or 3–4 ounces.) Using smaller plates can also help you decrease your portion sizes. The smaller the plate you serve your food on, the less food you will pile on.

When you serve yourself, be sure to fill half of your plate with veggies! This will help you get the vitamins, minerals, and fiber your body needs for optimal health. The other half of your plate should contain a lean protein or a whole grain option.

For more detailed information on portion sizes and how many calories you should be eating daily based on your age, sex, and level of physical activity, ask your healthcare provider, or go to ChooseMyPlate.gov and create a basic daily food plan based on your personal information.

2. Eat More Slowly

The more quickly you eat, the more weight you are likely to gain. When you eat fast, your body doesn't have enough time to receive, process, and send back the signals that tell you when you are already full. It takes about twenty minutes for your brain to register that your stomach is full. By eating more slowly, you are giving your body time to process the signals and let you know when you are full; as a result, you will eat less. Avoid eating while

watching TV because it's harder to pay attention to how fast you're eating. And always wait a few minutes before going back for seconds to be sure you really need them.

3. Drink 64 Ounces of Water throughout the Day

Drinking a lot of water is the one thing that every diet (and doctor!) recommends. Sixty-four ounces sounds like a lot, but trust us on this. It helps you feel fuller longer and makes for gorgeous, glowing skin to boot. Water eliminates food cravings and also helps prevent sugar cravings.

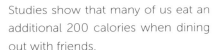

The Skinny on Dining Out

Studies show that many of us eat an additional 200 calories when dining out with friends.

When dining out, ask the waiter to portion half of your order *before* your meal is served and to bring you the other half in a to-go bag when you are ready to leave. This will help you to decrease your serving size and prevent mindless munching away long after you are full. Plus, you get a gourmet lunch already prepared for the next day!

Also, ask for food that is baked, grilled, or steamed and avoid added oils, fats, and butters. Season with lemon instead.

Try drinking a glass twenty minutes before eating so your body has time to absorb it. Make sure to drink upon awakening because that is when you are the most dehydrated, and always rehydrate after working out or spending time in the sun. Jené likes to add lemon juice to her water to give it a little natural flavor!

If you often forget to drink enough water, here's a tip that we learned from famed TV anchor Joan Lunden. Buy a pack of plastic bracelets, like the kind little girls wear. Put eight of them on one wrist. With each glass of water you drink throughout the day, transfer one bracelet to the other wrist. It's a fun and fashionable way to remind you to stay hydrated and keep track of how much you're drinking!

4. Stay Away from Refined Sugars, Sugar Substitutes, and Salt

Many experts are now suggesting that sugar is the leading force behind America's obesity epidemic, heart disease, and cancers. Sugar substitutes, some say, are also dangerous because they can increase cravings for regular sugar.

High salt intake increases blood pressure, which can lead to stroke, heart failure, and heart attacks. It also increases the risk of stomach cancer, osteoporosis, obesity, kidney stones, kidney disease, vascular dementia, and water retention! Try to stay away from table salt and get out of the habit of shaking it onto everything you eat. Adults should really not have more than 1 teaspoon of salt a day. (Most of the salt you eat is found hidden in processed foods under the name sodium chloride.) Himalayan pink salt is a much better option because it really packs a punch—so you need a lot

Fine-Tune Your Diet

One way to help fine-tune your diet is to get a blood test to determine if you have any food allergies or intolerances (it may or may not be covered by your health insurance). You will feel much better if you stay away from the foods that bring your body discomfort internally. Not everybody processes food the same way, so it's good to know the foods you should limit or avoid putting into your body.

less of it than regular table salt. It's one of the purest salts on earth and is naturally pink because of its high iron content. It also contains high amounts of trace minerals, which bring many health benefits. Surprisingly, it can be found at many grocery stores and it grinds just like sea or kosher salt.

5. Limit Alcohol Consumption

Have that glass of red wine at night; there are plenty of health benefits touted! Red wine has a high concentration of antioxidants called polyphenols, including resveratrol, that may improve and protect heart health by increasing the levels of high-density lipoprotein (HDL) cholesterol, which is considered the "good" cholesterol. It also reduces "bad" (LDL) cholesterol levels, which contribute to heart disease. However, avoid overindulging. Everything in moderation! It's recommended that women drink a maximum of one or two glasses, up to three or four times a week.

The 5 Basic Food Groups

There are five basic food groups in the Dietary Guidelines for Americans: fruits, vegetables, grains, dairy, and protein. We'll break down each of these groups below. And though they aren't major food groups, we will discuss healthy beverages, herbs and spices, and oils, because they provide essential nutrients.

Food not only makes you feel good, it also makes you look good! Here we'll also share the beauty bonuses that come from eating from each food group.

Fruit

Eat plenty and a wide variety. We suggest going fresh and organic when possible. When not possible, your next best choice is frozen, rather than canned. Canned fruit tends to be higher in sodium and sugar.

Fruit travels through the digestive tract much more quickly than other foods (within an hour!), so eating it on its own will give you the maximum nutritional benefits—even more so than combining it with vegetables in a juice or smoothie.

Fruits, and especially berries, contain high levels of anti-inflammatory and antioxidant agents, vitamins C and E, potassium, and magnesium, all of which help protect the body against environmental toxins and neutralize UV damage and free radicals (which can damage the DNA of healthy cells).

Beauty Bonus: Fruit can help stimulate collagen production, which helps with skin renewal to keep it firm and strong. Free radicals can accelerate premature aging (including wrinkle formation), so neutralizing these can help slow the visible effects of aging. Antioxidants support hair strength because they increase circulation to the scalp and support the tiny blood vessels that feed the hair follicles. Fruit also helps the body maintain healthy bones and

"If you keep good food in your fridge, you will eat good food."

—Errick McAdams

teeth; the vitamin D in some fruits improves calcium absorption.

Veggies

We suggest you eat a variety of dark green vegetables, especially dark leafy greens, as well as the brightest-colored veggies, such as ones that are red and orange. Try to always eat fresh and organic when possible. If fresh vegetables aren't in your budget, go with frozen rather than canned, just as with fruit. Frozen vegetables are sometimes even better for you than fresh vegetables because they are often picked at their peak, blanched, then flash frozen, so the nutrients are quickly locked in and not lost during the time spent in transport to the store.

Dark leafy greens are full of powerful antioxidants and vitamin K and are probably the most concentrated source of nutrition of any food. They, along with bright-colored veggies, are high in vitamins A, C, and E. Dark leafy greens contain folate, which is a water-soluble B vitamin that is key for cell growth and metabolism, especially during pregnancy. These vegetables are also rich in minerals such as iron, calcium, potassium, and magnesium, and contain a variety of phytonutrients including copper, lycopene, lutein, manganese (in the form of alpha-linolenic acid, or ALA), niacin, selenium, and zeaxanthin, which have protective and disease-preventing properties. These vegetables are packed with fiber as well, which benefits your heart health, weight management, and energy levels. Both dark leafy greens and bright veggies are also full of beta-carotene, which your body turns into vitamin A. This vitamin helps our cells to function properly and protects them from free radicals.

 Beauty Bonus: Eating dark leafy greens aids in weight loss, keeps you hydrated, and contributes to the health, growth, and repair of your skin, hair, and nails. It keeps hair follicles healthy and helps produce and circulate scalp oils. It provides natural protection against sun damage to your skin and hair, and the calcium in the greens will also give you healthy, strong bones and teeth and keep eyes bright. The beta-carotene in the greens protects against wrinkling and damage caused by UV rays and reduces inflammation to help with acne, making skin clearer.

Sea vegetables (often found in Asian cuisine) and fungi are also great foods to include in your diet. Sea vegetables are full of calcium, copper, iodine, iron, magnesium, manganese, omega-3 fatty acids, phytonutrients, potassium, selenium, and zinc. Mushrooms have been known to have many health benefits. They support your immune system and vitamin D levels, and also contain other powerful nutrients, vitamins, and minerals. They are also low in calories, fat-free, cholesterol-free, gluten-free, and low in sodium.

 Beauty Bonus: Fungi have been known to help with weight loss. And because they are rich in vitamin D, selenium, antioxidants, and anti-inflammatories, they help to protect your skin while also hydrating, healing, and providing anti-aging benefits. Fungi promote hair strength and growth as well.

Whole Grains

Grains are loaded with B vitamins to help with metabolism, and they contain other minerals like iron, magnesium, and selenium. The fiber in grains may help to reduce blood cholesterol levels and lower risk of heart disease, obesity, type 2 diabetes, and constipation. Eating fiber will also make you feel fuller longer.

Eating three servings of whole grains each day may help reduce the risk of some chronic diseases while providing nutrients that are vital to the health and maintenance of your body. Try eating whole grain rice, pasta, and breads, while avoiding the white variety flours or grains. If you have celiac disease or gluten sensitivity, opt for gluten-free foods.

 Beauty Bonus: The vitamin E and zinc in whole grains are great for hair and nail strength; the B and E vitamins and niacin are beneficial for healthy, sparkling eyes; the magnesium will contribute to strong teeth and bones; and the selenium will aid in nourishing and protecting the skin from sun damage.

Dairy

Opt for Greek yogurt, hard cheeses, and fermented dairy products, which are digested more easily. Some people even do better with raw dairy products (though be aware of the risks: raw milk products have not been pasteurized to kill harmful bacteria). Choosing raw, organic dairy from grass-fed or pasture-raised cows eliminates concerns like pesticides, hormones, antibiotics, and the effects of homogenization and pasteurization.

We also recommend choosing full-fat dairy. This goes against what many people believe to be healthy; low-fat dairy products are often recommended in recipes that claim to be better for you. But what we are learning now is that while whole milk has more calories than low-fat milk, it also has more of the healthy fat needed to digest the protein and absorb the calcium and vitamins you get from milk. Whole milk will also keep you feeling fuller longer, which may prevent you from snacking.

Keep in mind, however, that according to the National Digestive Diseases Information Clearinghouse, some 30 to 50 million Americans are lactose intolerant. Being lactose intolerant can cause digestive problems like nausea, cramps, bloating, gas, and diarrhea, usually beginning thirty minutes to two hours after eating or drinking foods containing the milk sugar lactose. Just know that for every dairy product, there is a dairy-free alternative. Some good dairy alternatives are soy-, rice-, and nut-based milks and cheeses. Not only do they *not* contain cholesterol, but they are also generally lower in fat and calories than their dairy counterparts.

If you are worried that by eliminating dairy you won't get enough calcium, potassium, protein, and fat, just know that you can get all of that from other food sources, like leafy green vegetables, fruits, beans, nuts, seeds, seaweed, and whole grains.

 Beauty Bonus: Use Greek yogurt as a skin mask to help heal acne-prone skin. Consuming it helps with hair, nail, and tooth growth and strength. It also helps to flatten your belly.

Protein

Grass-fed beef, free-range chicken, legumes, and fish are all good sources of protein. We recommend eating lean proteins.

Not only does filling up on protein make you feel fuller faster and longer, but your body also burns more calories to break down protein than to break down fats and carbohydrates. Want more good news? Protein accelerates weight loss from the mid-section first, and it is also the nutrient that builds muscle. The more muscle you have, the higher your metabolism is and the more fat your body will burn. The recommend serving size is 3.5 to 4 ounces.

 Beauty Bonus: Protein promotes healthy, strong hair and a healthy scalp. The iron in many protein sources helps cells carry oxygen to the hair follicles, and too little iron (anemia) is a major cause of hair loss.

 Beauty Bonus: Fish is great for skin, hair, and nail cell renewal and repair. It promotes the growth of strong, shiny, and hydrated hair, including your eyelashes, and helps to prevent hair loss. It aids in healthy, hydrated skin and scalp, and keeps your eyes healthy. It helps to fight inflammation that causes acne, premature aging, and irritation. It can also help reduce psoriasis symptoms and reduce the risk of non-melanoma skin cancer.

Make a Master Inventory Grocery List

To save time on regular grocery store trips, make a list of every grocery item you use in your home. You may even want to include the specific brands you use. When writing a shopping list, you can always pull from your master list after taking inventory of what you have or don't have. If you don't want to buy a particular product anymore, you can delete it from your master list. If you try something new that you or your family like, add it to your master list.

Keep a general shopping list near or in your pantry and add to it as you run out of a particular item, or add something to it that you want to try. This way, you are creating a list as you go, instead of having to spend time doing inventory later.

You may want to keep an updated general shopping list in your smartphone instead or as well, in case you are out and about and it's convenient for you to stop and get the things you need without having to go home to look first. With the smartphone, you can easily share this list with others you are delegating to as well. Try your best to just stick to your list when you're shopping. That will save you time and money. One great phone app for organizing and keeping track of your grocery lists is called SuperList. You can customize and share your list, upload pictures, and add pricing and quantity.

Beverages

Here are some recommendations for our favorite healthy beverages:

- Alkaline water: It may help to balance the body's pH levels.

- Water with lemon and/or cucumber: It helps flush the system.

- Coffee: The caffeine from that daily cup of coffee has been shown to help boost your energy, mood, memory, metabolic rate in fat burning, and liver function. It also reduces the risk of type 2 diabetes and effects of Parkinson's disease and has a positive effect on Alzheimer's.

- Organic unsweetened cranberry juice: It's great for urinary tract health.

- Organic green tea: The antioxidants in green tea reduce the effects of environmental skin damage from UV rays. They help prevent damage that can lead to cancer, and help skin repair itself. Green tea is also said to help speed metabolism and aid in weight loss.

- Organic white tea/herbal tea.

 Beauty Bonus: Coffee grounds can work as an excellent exfoliant, leaving soft, smooth skin. Some say it helps reduce cellulite when mixed with oil and massaged into the skin, and even reduces eye puffiness and dark circles. Try mixing some with coconut oil or extra-virgin olive oil!

Green tea is a great acne treatment! Place a steeped green tea bag directly on acne and hold there for a few minutes to allow the antioxidants to seep into the pores and get to work on helping clear up the blemishes.

Other Foods

DESSERT

Try having a piece of dark chocolate if you're craving something sweet. It contains as many polyphenols as red wine and is a potent antioxidant. Look for chocolate made of 70 percent or more cacao. The higher the cacao content, the higher the health benefits. Dark chocolate may improve blood flow and lower blood pressure, while fighting cardiovascular disease. Snacking on one piece a day not only curbs sweets cravings, it also stimulates endorphins, which make you happy! (We know it makes *us* happy!)

 Beauty Bonus: The antioxidants in chocolate help fight skin-damaging free radicals and protect the skin from sun exposure damage. Chocolate has anti-aging properties and helps keep skin moist and reduces roughness and scaling by increasing blood flow to the skin tissue. Ever tried a chocolate facial? It's a treat!

FATS AND OILS

Eat organic oils, like avocado, coconut, sesame, flaxseed, and extra-virgin olive oil, regularly in small amounts.

 Beauty Bonus: Oils act as anti-inflammatories, helping prevent premature aging, and contain antioxidants. They're great for healthy skin and help fight oxidative damage from the sun and pollution. Eating them helps hydrate your skin from the inside. Applying them on the outside, directly to your skin and hair, is an excellent intense moisturizing treatment.

NUTS AND SEEDS

Eat an ounce of raw organic nuts and seeds a day. Nuts contain fiber that helps promote regular bowel movements. The healthy fats in them help maintain brain function, nourish your red blood cells, fight excess inflammation, lower your cholesterol, and prevent diabetes and heart disease. They contain fat-soluble antioxidants that are also rich in biotin and vitamin E, which helps protect your cells from free-radical and DNA damage, and prevent cognitive decline as you age.

Seeds are the highest natural source of omega-3 fatty acids, which strengthen cell membrane barriers that allow water and nutrients in while keeping toxins out. They contain monounsaturated fatty acids and are full of fiber, antioxidants, protein, vitamin E, magnesium, manganese, phosphorus, and selenium. They help to lower cholesterol and reduce inflammation.

 Beauty Bonus: Nuts and seeds will keep your hair thick and shiny and protect your skin from the sun's damaging UV rays.

FRESH HERBS AND SPICES

Eat plenty of fresh herbs and spices, and use a wide variety to liven up your meals, awaken your senses, and provide you with long-term health benefits in a powerful little punch (or shall we say "pinch," because that's really all you need!).

Herbs and spices are rich in antioxidants and phytonutrients; they contain anti-inflammatory and anti-aging properties and aid in digestion and weight loss by boosting the metabolism. They have been used for hundreds of years to heal the body. Herbs and spices can replace fat, sugar, and salt in our food and even help to reduce our bloat. Spices have medicinal properties and can enhance not only the flavor of food but also its healing powers.

Shopping List

Pick what you like from the list; you don't have to buy everything all at once!

FRUIT
- apples
- berries (blackberries, blueberries, raspberries, strawberries)
- cantaloupe
- grapefruit
- kiwi
- lemons
- mangoes
- oranges
- papaya
- tomatoes

VEGETABLES
- arugula
- asparagus
- avocados
- bell peppers (red, orange, yellow, green)
- celery
- cucumbers
- eggplant
- kale
- radishes
- spinach

WHOLE GRAINS
- amaranth
- brown rice
- quinoa

DAIRY
- cottage cheese
- Greek yogurt
- hard cheeses (cheddar, Parmesan, etc.)
- kefir

PROTEIN
- albacore tuna, packed in water
- beans (kidney and black)
- beef, grass-fed
- chicken, free-range
- eggs, cage-free organic
- oysters
- white fish

NUTS AND SEEDS
- almonds (including natural almond butter)
- chia seeds
- flaxseeds
- pumpkin seeds
- sunflower seeds
- walnuts

FATS/OILS
- coconut oil
- extra-virgin olive oil
- grapeseed oil
- sesame seed oil

BEVERAGES
- alkaline water
- club soda
- coconut or almond milk
- coffee beans, whole or ground
- cranberry juice, unsweetened

- teas (organic chamomile, green, white, peppermint, spearmint)

HERBS AND SPICES
- basil
- cayenne pepper
- cilantro
- cinnamon
- "everything" spice with no sugar or MSG
- garlic
- ginger
- parsley
- Himalayan pink salt
- turmeric

CONDIMENTS
- apple cider vinegar, raw organic
- horseradish
- hot sauce
- mustard

SWEETENERS
- agave nectar
- coconut sugar
- honey, raw 100 percent pure
- maple syrup, Grade B, organic, and raw
- stevia

TREAT
- dark chocolate

Growing Your Own Herb Garden

Growing herbs is a fun experiment you can even involve your kids in. They will enjoy planting the seeds and watching your home garden grow. It can also teach them responsibility by giving them the task of learning to care for the plants by watering them when needed.

What to purchase:

- some of your favorite, most commonly used small herb plants from a local nursery
- small pots or containers that are around 6 to 12 inches deep
- a light potting mix (soil-less potting mix will avoid soil-borne diseases)
- fertilizer that is safe to use with edibles

Getting started:

1. Find a sunny window that gets at least five hours of sun per day and is away from drafts. If you don't have a sunny window, placed fluorescent lights about 18 inches from your plants for about ten hours a day.

2. Put a 2- to 3-inch layer of potting mix into the bottom of each pot or container.

3. Plant the herb plant in the container.

4. Fill the rest of the pot/container firmly with the potting mix, leaving about an inch at the top of the container for watering.

5. Lightly water the soil around the herbs—not the leaves directly—once daily. Don't drown them!

6. Once a week, feed your herbs with a light all-purpose fertilizer.

7. Watch for and remove damaged leaves and stems.

8. Trim your herbs often to encourage them to grow full and bushy.

9. Eat 'em!

Skinny Shopping

Shop skinnier and healthier! Here are some of our favorite easy-to-follow tips to incorporate on your new journey to a healthier you. Once you conquer one change, add in another tip from the list below on a weekly basis to a slimmer you!

- Don't go to the store when you're hungry. Sounds obvious, but you're more likely to grab junk food and make poor choices when your tummy is a-rumbling and your blood sugar level is low!

- Go armed with a list and don't stray from it. Stick to the week's meal plans and meal necessities.

- Stock up on fresh organic fruits and veggies if your budget allows, and if not, opt for bags from the freezer section to use in smoothies.

- Avoid packaged, processed, canned, prepared, and fast foods!

- Spend more time in the "outer aisles." This is typically where the healthier foods are stored.

- Don't buy any junk to keep at home. Bottom line: If it's not there, you can't eat it. This goes for the kids too. If your child has never tasted soda, when they're out and they have a choice, they usually won't choose it, because it has never been in the home.

How to Fit Healthy Eating into a Busy Lifestyle!

There are many simple ways to work healthy food into your life. This takes a little planning and prep work, but we promise that you will be thrilled with the convenient and abundant healthy snack choices. Whether it's a quick fix to have on the way to and from work, while playing chauffeur to your kids, on your way to the gym, between meetings, or on a road trip, these easy-to-make, healthy snacks will provide the fuel your body needs to help keep your metabolism going, with the bonus of producing healthy hair, skin, and nails.

21 Quick-Fix Grab-'n'-Go Options

1. Organic apples, oranges, clementines, peaches, grapes, and apricots

2. Half an avocado with fresh lemon juice, or sesame seed oil and seeds on it

3. Bowl of fresh berries (they are also good frozen and keep longer!)

4. Brown rice cake topped with almond butter

5. Celery sticks filled with organic raw almond butter—if you need a little extra zing, top it with a little drizzle of honey—or hummus (put them premade in storage bags into your refrigerator for easy grabbing)

6. String cheese or cubed hard cheese

7. Cottage cheese with pineapple

8. Smoothies (portion ingredients for single smoothies into freezer storage bags for future use; when you need a quick smoothie, all you have to do is dump the bag in your blender, add your healthy liquid of choice, blend, pour, and drink)

9. Peanut butter or almond butter (find individually portioned packages of peanut or almond butter to eat alone or with an apple, whole grain cracker, celery, or Jené's recent fave, a banana!)

10. Whey protein powder blended with a liquid (try it with water, coconut milk, or almond milk)

11. Canned light albacore tuna, alone or tossed over greens like arugula, with freshly squeezed lemon juice

12. Edamame (boil a half of a cup, sprinkle with a light amount of sea salt, and have as a snack or toss in a salad)

13. Greek yogurt with fresh berries drizzled with raw organic honey

14. 100 percent fruit puree pouches

15. Homemade trail mix of raw organic almonds, walnuts, pumpkin seeds, and sunflower seeds (put the mixture in plastic bags or in a jar for easy grabbing)

16. Roasted pumpkin seeds

17. Raw veggies (wash, chop, and divide all your vegetables for the week at once for easy grabbing; make bags of carrots, celery, broccoli, cauliflower, bell peppers, or radishes; have hummus available for dipping)

18. Hard-boiled organic cage-free eggs, eaten plain, in salads, or used to make egg salad sandwiches (boil a carton of organic cage-free eggs on a Sunday and store in the fridge to use as a quick, healthy protein snack during the week for you or the kids; leave the shells on and peel as you grab, or you can peel ahead of time, add sea salt, and put into a storage bag in the refrigerator to make it even more convenient)

19. Homemade fruit ice pops (blend your favorite fresh or frozen organic fruits with coconut milk and freeze in ice pop molds; Zoku has a great ice pop maker)

20. Homemade popcorn with olive oil and sea salt (when the popcorn has cooled, add salt, herbs, or Parmesan cheese to your liking and store it for a future grab-and-go snack)

21. 1 ounce of dark chocolate

You can portion out some of the above snacks for the week in plastic baggies or containers and keep in the fridge for quick and easy grabbing!

18 Quick Fixes for Belly Bloat

1. Take a probiotic supplement! Probiotics can restore bacterial balance, aid in digestion, and reduce excessive gas. You can also find probiotics in yogurt, kefir, and sauerkraut.

2. Stay hydrated so you'll release more body fluids and salt retained in the body. Drink a *lot* of water (about 64 ounces daily)!

3. Start and end your day with hot/warm water and lemon, or even add 1 tablespoon of organic apple cider vinegar. It will act as a natural diuretic and a gentle laxative that aids your body in losing water weight and bloat.

4. Avoid carbonated drinks. No sodas!

5. Increase potassium intake (lima beans are a good choice).

6. Cut sugar intake.

7. Reduce or eliminate alcohol consumption.

8. Try reducing or eliminating dairy and gluten (you might have an intolerance).

9. Eat raw ginger (you can also make a tea with it or soak raw slices in lemon juice), chew on raw garlic with honey, eat basil, and use turmeric (basil and turmeric are also excellent for relieving menstrual cramps). They all have antioxidant, antibacterial, and anti-inflammatory elements to help absorb the gas in the stomach and kill bacteria.

10. Eat celery, because it has a high water content and also contains nutrients that help rid your body of toxins.

11. Chew on a few fennel seeds or caraway seeds, parsley, or peppermint leaves after eating a big meal.

12. Take digestive enzymes.

13. Chew food more slowly to reduce swallowing a lot of air and also to allow the natural enzymes in your saliva to break down your food for easier digestion.

14. Try taking activated charcoal or a natural food enzyme known as alpha-galactosidase to help break down hard-to-digest foods.

15. Chew gum less. It causes you to swallow more air, which causes bloat.

16. Try drinking 1 teaspoon of baking soda dissolved in a small glass of warm water. You can also add a pinch of salt, and the juice of half a lemon to the glass.

17. Try detox or herbal teas with carminative herbs such as chamomile, cinnamon, coriander, fennel, ginger, peppermint, and spearmint. Steep for ten to fifteen minutes before drinking.

18. Eat freshly sliced pineapple. It contains bromelain, a digestive enzyme that helps break down food to help get rid of bloating.

Eating Like Royalty

Our fitness trainer, Jolene Matthews, suggests that we plan our meals like this:

1. **Eat breakfast like a king.** Eat within one hour of waking to amp up your metabolism and stabilize your blood sugar levels. Drink a cup of coffee or green tea (sans sugar) and then get in a

light workout on an empty stomach to burn stored fat. Afterward, eat a hearty meal of protein and good carbs. Eating like a "king" means this is the biggest meal of the day!

2. Eat lunch like a queen. Lunch should be a healthy salad chock-full of veggies and a protein like grilled chicken, or a protein plus a carbohydrate like brown rice.

3. Eat dinner like a pauper. Dinner should be a light source of lean protein and vegetables. Dr. Oz recommends not eating past 7 p.m. Your metabolism slows down later on in the day and especially in the few hours before retiring to bed. This means you cannot break down food as efficiently. Avoiding large meals at dinnertime is very effective in losing weight, particularly abdominal fat.

This may be counterintuitive to what you've traditionally done in the past (most people skip breakfast and eat a large dinner!), but trust us, it works!

Keep Your Motor Running

Get Encouragement from Friends

It's always great to have a friend or partner on the same health kick as you to call on for support and encouragement.

Keep a Food Journal

Journaling and logging your daily food intake and exercise keeps you accountable and aware of what you are consuming. We don't necessarily believe in "counting calories," however. As long as you are expending more calories than you are consuming on a daily basis, you are on the right track!

Manage PMS, Cramps, and Mood Swings through Lifestyle and Diet

- Take vitamin B6, calcium or magnesium, or primrose oil.
- Exercise regularly, three to five times per week.
- Eat regularly to maintain a more stable blood sugar level (every two to three hours).
- Limit intake of alcohol, caffeine, red meat, salt, and sugar.
- Don't smoke.
- Don't stress! Practice stress-reduction techniques. Take a relaxing hot bath, meditate, or try practicing biofeedback.
- Drink chamomile or ginger tea.
- Get six to eight hours of sleep.

Weigh In

For a lot of women, doing a daily or even weekly weigh-in helps them stay focused and aids in making needed adjustments to their diet. Had a slip or cheat meal? Get on the scale the next morning. This will provide the motivation you need to get back on track that very day. It will also help you to see which foods work for your diet goals.

When is the best time to weigh in? Your true weight is reflected in the morning before having anything—even a glass of water. Be sure to step on the scale wearing nothing but your birthday suit to get an accurate reading.

Send Yourself Reminder Alerts from Your Smartphone

Send yourself motivational messages to help stay conscious of making healthy eating choices. It can even be a reminder alert every two to three hours to eat a healthy snack to keep your metabolism going.

Jacqueline's Recipes
Super Salad

INGREDIENTS

1 (14-ounce) can garbanzo beans (chickpeas) or cannellini beans
½ pound shrimp, chopped
½ onion, chopped
2 cucumbers, chopped
2 tomatoes, chopped
2 avocados, peeled, pitted, and chopped
handful or two chopped green beans, steamed but firm
2–3 slices cooked bacon, chopped
handful chopped fresh parsley or cilantro

Dressing

juice of 1 lemon
apple cider vinegar
extra-virgin olive oil
salt and pepper

Combine all salad ingredients and toss. Then add lemon juice, apple cider vinegar, and olive oil to taste for a dressing, and season with salt and pepper to taste (or use a dressing of your choice).

I love the Good Seasons packet of Zesty Italian dressing that you make in the shaker. It's my favorite!

If you wanted to add some more greens, I would use chopped romaine hearts.

- -

Eggplant-Mozzarella Bruschetta

INGREDIENTS

1 large eggplant, sliced into ½-inch discs
2 eggs, beaten
1½ cups Italian bread crumbs
1 pound mozzarella cheese, sliced thinly to fit evenly over eggplant slices
6–8 fresh ripe Roma (plum) tomatoes, diced
1 onion, diced
2–3 large cloves garlic, minced
2 tablespoons chopped fresh basil
extra-virgin olive oil
balsamic vinegar
salt and pepper

Preheat oven to 350 degrees.

Dip eggplant slices in egg and coat with Italian bread crumbs. Fry in olive oil until golden brown (2–3 minutes on each side), drain excess oil on paper towel, then place on cookie sheet. Layer a thin slice of mozzarella cheese on top of each eggplant slice. Bake until cheese is melted (8–10 minutes).

In a bowl, combine tomatoes, onion, garlic, and basil. Toss with a little olive oil, salt, and pepper to taste. A little balsamic vinegar drizzled on top is a tasty touch!

Top baked eggplant slices with tomato mixture and serve.

This can also be eaten cold! And for a healthier option, grill the eggplant and skip the breading.

Turkey Soup

INGREDIENTS

olive oil
4 cloves garlic, thinly sliced
1 medium to large sweet yellow onion, diced
10 (14.5-ounce) cans chicken broth (Jacqueline prefers College Inn brand)
1 (5-pound) turkey breast, bone-in
6–8 medium to large carrots, chopped
6–8 celery ribs, chopped
4–8 oz. (½–1 cup) fresh white mushrooms, chopped
small handful chopped green onions
small handful chopped fresh parsley
generous pinch chopped fresh thyme
generous pinch chopped fresh marjoram
generous pinch chopped rosemary
1 bay leaf
garlic salt
pepper
½ lemon
Parmesan cheese

Add enough olive oil to coat the bottom of a large pot, add garlic and onion, and cook on medium to low heat until onion is almost translucent. Add chicken broth and whole turkey breast. Bring to a boil, then reduce heat to medium-low. When turkey is about cooked (about 1½–2 hours), remove and cut into bite-sized chunks, then return to pot along with the bone. Add the vegetables, parsley, thyme, marjoram, rosemary, and bay leaf.

When vegetables are cooked, add some garlic salt and fresh pepper (small pinch or to taste). Squeeze lemon into pot and drop in. Remove the turkey bone.

Serve with freshly grated Parmesan cheese.

You can also use diced green beans, tomatoes, peas, or whatever vegetable you like.

You can skip the chicken broth cans (and added sodium, as well as MSG) by just using the natural broth made by the turkey.

I like to change it up. You can separately add a small amount of pasta or rice, or even cubed cooked potatoes.

"The secret to reaching your fitness goals is getting started."

—Felicity Luckey

CHAPTER 5

Get Fit!

Getting fit is not just about looking good; it's imperative for a healthy lifestyle.

This chapter will help you understand your body type and fitness goals, and then give you ways to get in better shape, no matter what your schedule looks like. We'll talk about cardio and strength training, share some of our favorite stretching and toning routines, and share the best exercises to target the trickiest areas.

Since we love staying fit and healthy but we aren't certified fitness trainers, we've brought in experts and personal trainers Jolene Matthews and Samanta Bianco to help out with aspects of this chapter.

Whether it's squeezing in walking lunges while holding your baby, squats and calf raises in front of your stove while cooking, a quick power walk around the block on your lunch break, or bicep curls with your full basket at the grocery store, even the busiest women can squeeze in a few minutes a day to *get fit*!

Your Body and Your Fitness Goals

There is beauty in everything and in everyone, no matter your shape or size! Why do we tend to notice the beauty in others, but not in ourselves? We always seem to want something we don't have—never content with what we've got.

A long and lean woman may want that curvaceous hourglass shape, while the hourglass-shaped woman wishes she were leaner, with smaller hips. Small-busted women want larger breasts, while big-busted women want smaller ones. Shorter women wish they could be taller, while taller women wish they were more petite . . . and so on. You know the saying: the grass is always greener on the other side.

And almost all of us want to be thinner. But keep in mind that just because someone *appears* thin, it doesn't necessarily mean they are healthy or

"To me, beauty is about being comfortable in your own skin. It's about knowing and accepting who you are."

—Ellen DeGeneres

fit—and sometimes, it's not *thinner* we want to be, just *more toned.* Our advice to you is not to strive to be a size 2. Instead, strive for being the healthiest you can, from the inside out—and get ready to reap the amazing benefits that come with that.

Sometimes all we need is a just a little fine-tuning to look and feel better than ever. There is always room for improvement, and nothing should stop you from striving to look the best that *your* body can look, or from feeling great and confident about yourself.

Your Body Type

Understanding your body type is a great first step in creating a fitness plan because it can show you where you tend to gain weight and help you determine what exercises will best balance your body proportions. (It's also beneficial in helping you choose clothes that most flatter your shape—but more about that in chapter 9!)

When determining your body type, please keep in mind that none of these body types are better than the other. The "perfect" body type is a matter of perception. What someone finds ideal or desirable is a matter of opinion, and very individual. So whether you realize it or not, you've already *got it!* Get it?

RECTANGLE

Are you tall and slender? Is the width across your shoulders the same as your hip width? Are you long in the waist without a lot of curves? Then you're a rectangle.

Celebrity example: Taylor Swift

Fitness focus: Consider adding some muscle tone to your already long, lean, and slender shape. Do some all-over strength- and weight-training exercises to tone and build those muscles to give you some extra curves.

"I think that whatever size or shape body you have, it's important to embrace it and get down! The female body is something that's so beautiful. I wish women would be proud of their bodies and not dis other women for being proud of theirs!"

—Christina Aguilera

SQUARE

Similar to a rectangle, but with a shorter waist. If you're a square, you probably have more of an athletic build.

Celebrity example: Jessica Alba

Fitness focus: Try doing stretching and lengthening exercises to lean your look. Yoga would be a great addition to your workout!

TRIANGLE

Do you have narrow shoulders, a small chest, and wider hips? Is your bottom half your widest part? Do you struggle with saddlebags and thicker thighs? Baby got back? Then this is your shape.

Celebrity example: Beyoncé

Fitness focus: Balance your body: Try upper-body strength-training exercises to build more arm muscle, plus variations of leg lifts for inner and outer thigh toning to slim your bottom half.

INVERTED TRIANGLE

Do you have wide shoulders, possibly a big chest, narrow hips, and thin legs, with little definition in the waist? Is your top half your widest part? Then this is you. You most likely have an athletic build.

Celebrity example: Jessica Simpson

Fitness focus: You can slim your arms and shoulders by using lighter weights with a full range of movements, while building a little booty with some squats and lunges. Side bends and stretching can help slim the waist.

HOURGLASS

Is the width of your shoulders the same width as your hips? Do you have a narrow and clearly defined waist? Do you consider your thighs to be a little fuller? Do you have a curvaceous backside? Then you're an hourglass.

Celebrity example: Kim Kardashian

Fitness focus: Do equal upper- and lower-body sculpting workouts; don't overwork one area more than the other. You want to stay balanced. Cardio is also good for you!

DIAMOND

Do you have narrow shoulders, with larger breasts and wider hips and waist? Do you carry most of your weight around your middle section, and have thinner arms and calves? Then you're a diamond. You probably tend to gain weight in your hips, belly, back, and buttocks.

Celebrity example: Oprah

Fitness focus: Focus on core exercises like side bends, planks, and crunches. Pilates is a great core workout and will help you get a longer, leaner, more flexible body. Equal strength training on upper and lower body will also help to balance you out. Cardio will help burn off that middle!

ROUNDED

Are your shoulders and hips wide and rounded? Is your waist/midsection your widest part? Do you have a soft middle? Are you big-breasted with a voluptuous figure? Your shape is rounded.

Celebrity example: Adele

Fitness focus: If you're looking to lose weight, a high-intensity cardio workout is a must! You can also add a full-body conditioning routine to build more muscle (also a great way to help burn fat).

How You See Yourself

Grab a notebook or open a text document and write down your body type. Now make a couple of lists underneath that:

Yoga Mom

Jacqueline is a big fan of yoga—it's great for every body type. It strengthens that mind-body-spirit connection we all need. It keeps you flexible, strong, and lean and encourages your organs to keep working smoothly. It also reduces stress.

List #1: Make a list of all your positive body attributes. What do you love about yourself? Do you have shapely legs, toned arms, pretty feet, or great breasts? List all the body parts that you feel good about, from head to toe! Don't leave anything out!

List #2: Make a list of all the things about your body you would like to see look different or make improvements on, if you had the power to change *any*thing about yourself.

Look closely at List #2. First, circle *only* the things you actually have control over and do have the power to change. Do you wish you could lose a little weight across your midsection? Would you like to have a firmer behind or more definition and tone on your arms? Those are examples of things you can control.

Next, cross out all the things that you don't have the power to change about yourself—and work on adding them to the list of things you love about yourself.

Instead of wishing for changes in areas you can't control, learn to accept and embrace the attributes you have. The facts are, you are not going to grow taller, get shorter, grow a longer waist, or get curvaceous if you are physically built to be long and lean. These are things you do not have control over. But you do have control over how you perceive them, positively or negatively. There is beauty in how you were made, so allow yourself to see that in yourself and be proud! There is always going to be someone that is wishing for exactly what you are already blessed with. Practice saying, "I love my _____" until you actually do!

Commit to Be Fit (8 to Great!)

A workout routine can be tough to start and tougher to keep up. These eight tips will help keep you on track.

Key #1: Know the Benefits of Exercise!

Exercise is essential to losing weight, getting stronger, attaining more energy, and sleeping better! Don't consider getting fit an option; think of it as a necessity.

Your overall health affects just about every area of your life. Think about how much easier physical chores would be if they didn't result in stiffness or aches and pains. Think of the energy and effort it takes to keep up and play with your children, or even your active pets, if you have them! Even sex can improve with being more fit! And, of course, you will feel better in your clothes and even find more things to wear when you shop your closet!

Key #2: Create Desire and Motivation for Change!

Ask yourself why you want to be fit. Are there certain clothes you are longing to fit into? Is your level of fitness, or lack thereof, making daily activities difficult, because of either your physical limitations or a lack of energy? Is your current body or fitness state holding you back from something important you want in your life?

Whatever your reasons for being ready to commit and whatever your driving force is for change, consider writing them down somewhere that lets you remind yourself of them often!

Key #3: Make Fitness Goals Easy to Reach!

Don't resolve to lose 30 pounds in three weeks. (Fitness expert Jolene Matthews actually recommends not aiming to lose any more than 2 to 2½ pounds per week.) Instead, focus on short-term fitness goals, like making positive choices daily. Don't look too far ahead. The results will come!

Why Losing Weight Is Less Important Than Gaining Muscle

Jolene actually tells us not to focus on losing weight at all, because muscle weighs more than fat. As you build muscle, it will help burn fat, so while you lose inches, you may not always lose many pounds.

Key #4: Write Down Your Fitness Goals!

List your individual goals somewhere you can easily refer back to them and view them often. Do you desire more toned arms? A firmer behind? Make a vision board with what you want to look like and look at it daily.

Please keep in mind, though, that a lot of the images of people in magazines are altered to smooth out imperfections and slim down overall. Photoshop is a tricky thing! Use the visuals to motivate you and keep you going, but don't get too caught up on "perfection." Have realistic expectations, and just strive for the best body that your body can be!

Key #5: Customize Your Fitness Routines!

Put together a plan of action for what your daily workouts will look like. Create a playlist of some of your favorite motivational songs to work out to. Pick a TV show on Netflix that you will watch only during your walk on the treadmill—trust me, you will look forward to walking! Pick out some cute workout outfits you will feel good in, to get you in the zone.

Key #6: Schedule the Time for Your Workouts!

Find the times during your day where you have gaps in your schedule, and add your workouts to your schedule as you would any other appointment or meeting. You might even want to set reminder alerts on your smartphone. One option: Get up an hour earlier to fit in your stretches or cardio.

Key #7: Follow Through!

Stick to the plan! Don't think, just do it! Commit to actions that work for you and your schedule and keep moving forward. Allow your workout to become as much of a habit as brushing your teeth. If you work out in the morning, lay out your workout outfit and fill up your water bottle the night before so you'll remember and you'll be ready to go when you wake up.

Key #8: Maintain Your Drive and Determination!

You can do this by reading over your motivation, goals, and action plan often and by regularly looking at your vision board. Or stand naked in front of your mirror more often. That will keep you moving! The more results you see, the better you'll start to look and feel, the more energized you will become, and the more you will feel motivated to keep with it.

Fitness Tips from Jolene Matthews

Our ancestors were so much more active than we are today. They were up at the crack of dawn, working the land, farming, hunting, and walking for miles to and from school, work, and church. Today we lead much more stationary lives. Luckily, it doesn't take much to change your mind-set, your energy levels, your stamina, your body shape, and your life!

Just by becoming more active, individuals who are severely overweight or obese can significantly lower their risk for developing serious health problems, regardless of age. Studies show that excess fat around the waist is linked to diabetes, heart problems, and even some types of cancer.

Whether you are looking to shed 5 pounds or 50, keep in mind—and I apologize for my rigorous honesty here, ladies—there is no magic pill or quick fix. It's going to take work and dedication, as with anything else we achieve in life. Even with plastic surgery (liposuction, tummy tuck) or a gastric bypass, you *still* have to continue to eat healthy and work out; otherwise, you just gain the weight back (and then some).

So take it slow and enjoy the process. Make your fitness action plan doable by beginning with fairly easy changes. However small you start, you'll see gradual but important changes in your body and the way you feel.

Maybe you have low energy and find exercise exhausting; you may feel fatigued at the very thought of it. But if you keep it up and exercise more, your stamina will quickly increase. The pounds will come off, more intense workouts will become easier, and you may even want to do more!

—*Jolene*

Here are Jolene's easy-to-follow tips to incorporating fitness into your daily life.

Please note: It's important to consult your doctor before starting up a new exercise routine.

1. **Go to the gym and ask for a complimentary personal training session.** This will help you to learn your way around the club and the machines and learn correct form for each exercise.

2. **Make your immediate goals eating a well-balanced, healthy diet and doing cardio-based exercises.** This will help you to lose excess weight first. Choose high-intensity interval training (HIIT) cardio workouts—workouts where you alternate very intense bouts of exercise with lower-intensity exercise. Example: a 30-second sprint followed by a 60-second walk, repeated 5 to 10 times. This maximizes your time and effort because HIIT

has been shown to increase your metabolism for hours after working out.

3. **Work out regularly, including 30 minutes a day minimum of cardio or strength training.** Even a daily speed walk around the block counts.

4. **Load up on water.** Drink water before, during, and after exercise to maintain hydration. Dehydration can affect coordination and cause muscle fatigue and cramping. Plus, proper hydration helps regulate body temperature to avoid overheating.

5. **Warm up.** Doing a quick warm-up increases your heart rate and blood flow to the muscles you will be working on, which will loosen them up and help prevent injuries. A warm-up also helps you to mentally prepare for your workout. Something like 5 minutes of jumping jacks is all you need.

6. **Cool down.** Cooling down brings your heart rate down, helps you resume your normal breathing, and prevents dizziness, injuries, and soreness.

7. **Begin and end every exercise routine with at least a 5-minute stretch.** This helps warm up and cool down the body, plus increases flexibility and helps prevent injury.

8. **Mix up your fitness routine.** Alternate through different forms of exercise to work different muscle groups and prevent your

Take Your Kids to the Gym

Many gyms nowadays offer daycare services so the kids can play while mom commits to getting fit!

muscles from getting complacent—muscles "remember" workouts and adapt quickly. They no longer have to work as hard and your results quickly diminish. Switching things up will also keep you from getting bored. Most people plateau because they are doing the same thing (like the elliptical or treadmill) week after week.

Make Fitness a Family Affair

Think you don't have time to work out because of the kids? There are plenty of ways to include them that are fun for them, too!

- Take a hike.
- Explore the neighborhood.
- Go on a bike ride.
- Roller-skate or Rollerblade.
- Have a race to see who can run the fastest.
- Play a team sport with the family.
- Canoe, paddle-boat, or kayak together.
- Play Twister (it's great for strength, stretching, and balance).

9. **Workouts should increase weekly in both time and intensity.** Don't hit a fitness plateau. Continue to challenge yourself.

10. **Find a workout partner, personal trainer, or group fitness class.** Did you know eight out of ten people who join a health club see no changes in their shape after six months? This is because they are usually doing it on their own. A workout partner or trainer will help keep you accountable and push you toward your fitness goals in the shortest amount of time possible. And I am a huge fan of group fitness. A great instructor and fun music can get anyone excited about working out—plus these professionals are constantly changing up their already intense routines.

Jolene's Quickie At-Home, Full-Body Workout

I know not every woman has the luxury of a trainer and/or an expensive gym membership—or the time and stamina to hit the gym seven days a week even if she does—so we'll focus on things you can do all on your own and on your own time! Here's my effective and quick fitness workout plan to get you more results in less time.

—*Jolene*

Each exercise here and throughout the chapter is demonstrated by fitness trainer Samanta Bianco.

1. Planks

Begin on hands and knees with shoulders directly over your wrists. Tuck your toes under and extend your legs directly behind you. Drop to forearms and keep neck and head aligned with your spine. Pull stomach muscles in and don't allow your back to drop or sag. Your body should form a straight line from your heels to the top of your head. Hold pose for at least 30 seconds; increase as you get stronger.

2. Push-Ups

Start in plank position, shoulders in line with wrists, and lower your body down to the floor, keeping movements slow and controlled, then push yourself up to starting position. Repeat until you can no longer hold your form or lift yourself off the floor.

3. Jump Lunges

From a standing position, with your hips aligned forward, tighten your core and step forward into a lunge with front leg bent to a 90-degree angle, making sure the knee does not extend over the toes. Springing off your feet, jump up while switching legs in a scissor motion, landing on heel to toe in a lunge with the opposite leg. Repeat 10 times.

4. Burpees

Start in a squat position, back flat and legs bent at a 90-degree angle, with knees not extending over the toes. Place your hands on the floor and kick your legs back to push-up position. Do a push-up, then jump forward to your hands and spring upward and into a jump squat. Try to repeat 20 times.

5. Wall Squat

Stand with your back against a wall, then step your feet out in front of you and lower your body until your legs are at a 90-degree angle. Hold a medium-size ball (like a soccer or basketball) between your thighs and squeeze it as tight as you can. Hold for 30 seconds, and then stand. Repeat 4 times.

"You don't get the ass you want by sitting on it."

6. Squat, Bicep Curl, Overhead Press

From a standing position, hold dumbbells down at your sides. Go into a squat. On the way up to a standing position, do a bicep curl. Once standing, in one constant fluid motion, turn wrists so palms are facing inward as you push your arms upward and then facing forward as you reach full arm extension above your head. Go back down in reverse order. Do 3 sets of 10 to 15.

Jacqueline's Favorite Stretch Routine

Wake up and prepare for bed each day with a stretch to lengthen those muscles and increase your flexibility!

Stretch #1: Big Arm Circles

1. Stand with feet shoulder width apart and head and spine in alignment (stomach held in and sit bone slightly tucked under).

2. Reach arms up as high as you can, with the inside of your elbows facing your ears and hands facing each other, while reaching up and out of your body.

3. Hold for a few seconds.

4. Turn hands facing away from each other, and in one sweeping wide movement, move arms straight back, down, and to your sides.

5. Then crisscross them in front of your body to complete the circle, and return to holding your arms straight above the head with palms facing each other.

6. Do 10 circles in this direction, then 10 circles in the opposite direction (cross, down, then up). Always reach upward and outward as much as possible. Try to go through the full range of motion to feel the stretch and don't race through it. Move at a slow and controlled pace.

Stretch #2: Side Bend

1. Stand with head and spine aligned and one arm stretched upward, palm facing in. Place the other hand on the hip bone.

2. Reach up and out of your body as high as you can, then bend at the waist to the opposite side of whichever hand you have raised, reaching up and over as far as you can. Stay in perfect alignment while keeping that arm up straight and close to the side of your head.

3. Once you have bent over as much as you can, make small, controlled half-inch pulses toward the opposite side, to a count of 100.

4. Slowly reach up with both hands, palms and elbows in, drop the opposite hand to your hip bone, and do another count of 100 to the other side.

5. Return to hands-above-head position.

Stretch #3: Forward Bend

1. Grasp opposite arms above the elbows (on the biceps) in front of you.

2. Lift your grasped forearms to meet your forehead, then, with feet hip distance apart, bend forward with a straight back as far as you can without curving your back or locking your knees.

3. Hold as long as you can, up to 60 seconds.

4. Then release into a relaxing, hanging, upside-down position while holding on to the outside of your ankles and pulsing slowly, pulling your head toward your legs, to a count of 20.

Stretch #4: Three-Part Front Split Stretch

1. Do a runner's lunge: With your hands on the floor, keep one foot flat between your hands, knee at a 90-degree angle, while the other leg is straight behind you, resting on the ball of the foot with heel reaching back.

2. Hold for 30 seconds.

3. Shift your weight backward and onto your back leg, straightening both legs and flexing your front toes upward.

4. Keeping your back flat, lean in toward the front leg to feel the stretch.

5. Hold for 30 seconds.

6. Place the front toes back on the ground and slide into the split position as far as you can go and hold for 30 to 60 seconds.

7. Switch legs and repeat steps 1 through 6 on the other side.

Stretch #5: Three-Part Seated Straddle Stretch

1. Sit on floor in a straddle-leg position, toes pointed and turned out, with straight legs.

2. Reach up with both arms as high as you can, reaching up and out of your body, then bend forward with flat back.

3. Place your hands on your shins or your ankles as far forward as you can reach.

4. Hold for a count of 60 to 100.

5. Facing forward, reach one arm up and over your body toward the opposite leg, bending your torso to the side. (If you are flexible enough, you can slide the pinkie finger of the first hand between your big and middle toe, in a karate chop position, as you reach the other arm over.)

6. Do little pulses for 60 to 100 counts.

7. Turn your body until your chest faces your leg and, with arms stretched upward, slowly bend over as far as you can while keeping a flat back, placing your hands flat on the ground on either side of your leg or foot, depending on your flexibility.

8. Hold for 60 to 100 seconds.

9. Repeat steps 5 through 8 on the other side.

Stretch #6: Seated Forward Bend

1. Starting in a seated position, bring both legs straight out in front of you, flat on the ground, with feet flexed and toes up.

2. Reach up to the ceiling and then bend forward toward your toes as far as you can, keeping a flat back. Hands should either hold on to the balls of your feet or be placed on your shins.

3. Gently try to get your forehead to touch your legs and hold for 60 seconds.

Stretch #7: Reclined Split Stretch

1. Lie flat on your back, keeping legs straight on floor, toes pointed.

2. Lift one leg, grab your calf or ankle (or hook a band, belt, or a rolled towel around the arch of your foot), and pull your leg toward your head using your hands.

3. Keep leg straight, lifted out of your body, and toes pointed, with the other leg firmly planted on the ground as you pulse the working leg toward your head for 60 seconds.

4. Repeat steps 1 though 3 on the other leg.

5. Grab big toes with pointer and middle fingers, or use a band, towel, or even a scarf wrapped around the arch of your foot (depending on your flexibility), and pull legs open and out to either side for small controlled pulses for 60 seconds.

Stretch #8: Backbend

1. Lie on your back with feet hip distance apart, knees bent, feet flat on ground.

2. Place your hands on the floor on either side of your head, fingers facing toward your feet.

3. Arch your back and roll onto the top of your head, then try to lift your head up off the floor into a backbend.

4. If this is all that you can do, hold it right there. If you are more flexible, push head up and off the ground using your arms into more of an arched back.

5. Hold for 30 seconds. Do 3 sets.

Stretch #9: Standing Forward Bend

1. With legs together and arms at your sides, exhale as you reach your arms up, then bend forward at the hips (not the waist), bringing your head toward your knees. Let the crown of your head hang down toward the floor, keeping your heels pressed into the floor. Do not lock your knees!

2. Hold for 20 seconds.

3. Stand up and reach your arms straight above your head as high as you can, palms in, returning to your starting position.

4. Breathe in as deep as you can and exhale, lowering your arms down to your side.

You can also add stretches to target more specific muscle groups like triceps, quads, and glutes, and end with some neck rolls.

Find Your Cardio Style

Don't feel chained to the treadmill every day. There are lots of other activities that provide the same cardiovascular benefits. We've tried everything from pole fitness to hot yoga—the important thing is to find things you can enjoy doing at least thirty minutes a day, four to five times a week!

Try the suggestions that follow to find out what's right for you!

Brisk Walking (aka the Power Walk)

Walk with a friend. Use hand or wrist weights, or push a stroller for resistance. Walk fast and squeeze your buttocks muscles while walking, which will isolate those muscles and make them work even harder!

415 calories per hour

Running/Jogging

Running is a great way to burn fat and strengthen your core and leg muscles. Plus, no pricey gym membership needed!

Start with a slow jog for a mile and build up to faster sprints, for longer distances. Switch it up by adding light hand weights on some days, and even add walking lunges.

398 calories per hour for jogging, more for running

Biking

Get some fresh air while strengthening your heart, firming your legs, and lifting your behind.

483 per hour, depending on your speed and resistance

Dance

Zumba, hip-hop, ballroom, country line dancing, or freestyle—whatever kind of class calls to you. You can even put on your best song playlist at home and dance like nobody is watching . . . because they're not!

370 calories per hour

Kickboxing

Get some aggression out and learn a new skill, all while you burn fat and calories. Over time, kickboxing vastly improves coordination and posture. And boxing on the bag is the ultimate workout for burning fat (especially around the belly) and toning both upper and lower body.

650 calories for a 45-minute class

Jump Rope

Jumping rope targets about every muscle in the body, but your core really reaps the benefits, since it's working hard to stabilize your entire body as it moves through the air.

10 calories per minute

Jolene's Guide to Strength Training

The workout that is most effective at changing your shape, if performed correctly and consistently, is strength training. Jené is a perfect example of this—she went from a size 12 to a size 2 in under two years with consistent weight training, and changed her shape from curvy to athletic in the process. It can be done!

Many women are intimidated by going to the gym. And that's assuming they have the budget or access! If you can't make it to the gym or choose not to, you can also purchase some inexpensive free weights, anywhere from 3 to 15 pounds, or use items found around the home, like full soup cans or water bottles filled with sand, rocks, or change. (Keep in mind that you can also perform many exercises at home without weights by using your own body weight as resistance.)

Baby Weight

Trying to lose a few pounds and rebuild your strength post-pregnancy? Your baby makes a great weight! Try carefully squatting in place while holding your infant (in a carrier or in a sling works too).

1. **Eat before you lift.** The meal you eat before a strength-training workout (remember to wait two hours!) should be a 4:1 ratio of carbs to protein. This ratio ensures your body can replenish glycogen stores and repair tissue that you are breaking down during your workout.

2. **Form over reps.** Don't rush your workout. Every rep needs to be performed slowly and accurately so that the resistance goes to the right muscle groups and so you can avoid injury. Keep your reps slow and controlled on the way up as well as on the way down.

3. **Go heavy or go home.** Many women think that they will get too big or "bulky" if they lift heavy weights. Truth is, you bulk up because you are eating too many calories! Your diet has to complement your strength training.

   All women want to focus on "toning" and think that's the only point of weight training. However, building up muscles makes your body a lean, mean, fat-burning machine that keeps on working and burning calories even while you are at rest.

   Don't be afraid to go heavier. You will get stronger and reap the benefits of a sculpted physique in a shorter amount of time.

4. **Minimize breaks.** Take no more than a 60-second rest between sets. To maximize fat and carbohydrate burning, you don't want to let your heart rate or body temperature drop.

5. **Repetition counts.** Shoot for 3 sets of 12 to 15 reps of each exercise per session.

6. **Work opposing muscle groups on the same day.** Opposing muscle groups are ones that perform opposite movements—one muscle strengthens while the other muscle lengthens. Working them out to increase overall flexibility and strength together means the muscles will be balanced; an imbalance can cause injury. Be sure to train large muscle groups at each workout, and switch up the muscle group you train each day. For example:

> *Mondays:* chest (pectoralis major) and back (trapezius/rhomboideus, latissimus dorsi, erector spinae)

> *Tuesdays:* arms (biceps, triceps) and shoulders (deltoids)

> *Wednesdays:* legs (quadriceps, hamstrings), calves, and butt (gluteus maximus)

> *Thursdays:* repeat Monday workout

> *Fridays:* repeat Tuesday workout

> *Saturdays:* repeat Wednesday workout

> *Sundays:* rest day

7. **Get six to eight hours of sleep every night.** Your muscles will have an easier time repairing and rebuilding while your body is at rest!

—Jolene

Strength Training to Target Specific Problem Areas

Back Fat, Bra Bulge, and Arm Fat Blasters

1. Push-Ups

Start in plank position, shoulders in line with wrists, and lower your body down to the floor, keeping movements slow and controlled, then push yourself up to starting position. Repeat until you can no longer hold your form or lift yourself off the floor.

Target areas: Chest, back, arms, stomach

See pictures on page 59.

2. Tricep Dips

Sit on a bench or stable chair, legs either bent or stretched out in front of you on the floor, and place hands on either side of your hips, fingertips pointing forward. Move your bottom forward off the bench and lower hips toward the floor. Then by pressing through the heel of the palm, lift yourself back up again. Try to do 3–4 sets of 20 reps each.

Target area: Triceps

3. Kickbacks

Hold a dumbbell in your right hand and assume a split stance position (place left leg forward with weight evenly distributed between both feet). Contract your abs to support your lower back and lean forward to flat back position. Square your shoulders and bend elbow to 90 degrees, extending your arm at the elbow while squeezing the tricep. Do 1 set of 15 to 20 reps and then switch and do the other arm. Complete 3 sets of 15 to 20, alternating on each arm.

Target area: Triceps

4. Bicep and Hammer Curls

Bicep curl:

Hold a dumbbell in each hand in a standing position with palms facing forward, then bend your elbows and lift dumbbells up toward your shoulders without lifting palms higher than the shoulder line.

Release your arms back down to your sides. Do 3 sets of 15 to 20.

Hammer curl:

When you have finished the sets, turn your hands so that your palms face in toward your body and repeat 3 sets of 15 to 20 using the same form.

Target area: Biceps

5. Chest Flys

Lie down on your back on a flat bench and, holding dumbbells, extend your arms into the air with palms facing in. Keeping elbows slightly bent, lower weights to slightly higher than the shoulder line. Squeezing the chest, bring weights back up to starting position. Do 3 sets of 15.

Target areas: Chest, arms, armpit bulge, shoulders

6. Bent-Over One-Arm Dumbbell Rows

Standing, with your right leg firmly planted on the floor, bend your left knee and place it and your right hand firmly on a flat bench. You should be bent over, with back parallel to the floor. Your right hand should serve as support for your body. Maintaining a tight core and flat back, contract your lats and biceps, and slowly row the dumbbell upward until it's above your torso. Hold for a moment, then slowly lower the dumbbell to a full extension—you should feel a stretch throughout your upper back. Do 3 sets of 15 and then repeat on other side.

Target areas: Shoulders, lats, back

Belly and Muffin-Top Blasters

1. The Pilates 100

Lie on your back in neutral spine position, lift feet and knees off the floor, with legs up and bent at a 90-degree angle, shins parallel to the floor. (As you get stronger you can straighten and lower your legs, keeping them together with toes pointed outward.) Inhale, palms facing forward, as you reach your arms up to the ceiling. Exhale as you lift your head off the ground, chin tucked in, and roll until your shoulder blades are off the floor as you lower your straight arms toward the floor, reaching toward the wall. The lower back should not come off the floor. Inhale for 5 short breath counts in as you pump your arms up and down in 6-inch movements, then exhale for 5 short breath counts out the same way (try saying shh, shh, shh, shh, shh in a forced breath as you exhale). Continue breathing counts for 10 full breaths for a total of 100 breath counts.

2. Bicycle

Lying down with lower back flat on the floor, place fingertips behind the head with elbows extended out to the sides. Reach one elbow to the bent opposite knee while extending the other leg straight out about 6 inches above the floor. Repeat on other side. The closer the leg is to the floor, the more challenging the exercise will be. Aim for 20 reps.

3. Stamp and Lower

While lying on your back, make a triangle shape with your thumbs and forefingers and place your hands under your tailbone, palms on the floor. Extend legs up toward the ceiling, keeping legs straight and together, then lower them to a few inches above the ground. Raise them back to starting position, then try to lift your hips off the ground as if you are trying to stamp the ceiling with the soles of your feet. Lower hips to the ground and lower the legs. Repeat for 10 reps.

4. Traditional Crunch

Lying down with lower back flat on the floor and knees bent, feet flat on the floor, place fingertips behind the head with elbows extended out to the sides. Lift chin up to the ceiling as you lift shoulder blades off the floor. Squeeze abs at the top of the movement and then lower back down to starting position. Be careful not to pull on the neck to lift yourself up. Aim for 25 reps.

Inner Thigh Jiggle Blasters

1. Leg Squeeze

Sitting in front of a bench or stable chair, put the arches of your feet on the outside of the chair's legs or something sturdy about hip distance apart. Squeeze your legs inward as hard as you can. Keep squeezing continuously for 100 counts. Release.

"Good things come to those who sweat."

2. Inner Leg Lift

Lie on your side on the floor, propped up with one arm, hips stacked on top of each other, bottom leg straight with top leg bent in front of you, knee pointing toward the ceiling and foot flat on the floor. Flex the foot on the extended leg, keeping toes facing forward, and arch toward the ceiling. Lift and lower the leg, keeping it straight and taking it up as high as you can go, for 2 counts up and 2 counts down. Do this 30 times. Repeat on the other side.

Booty and Saddlebag Blasters

1. Leg Lifts and Fire Hydrant Leg Lifts

Leg Lifts:

Start on the floor on your hands and knees. Stretch one leg straight back behind you, foot pointed. Keep abs held in and don't let your back droop. Lift and lower straight leg 20 times, making sure to squeeze your glutes at the top of the lift, then finish with 20 quick pulses upward from the top of the lift. Next, bend the knee with foot flexed and push up toward the ceiling. Lift and lower leg 20 times then again finish with 20 quick pulses upward from the top of the lift. Repeat on other leg.

Fire Hydrant Leg Lifts:

Staying on all fours, move the first leg straight out to the side, toes pointed. Lift and lower leg 20 times, then finish with 20 quick pulses upward from the top of the lift. Bend your knee 90 degrees and lift and lower the leg another 20 times, again finishing with 20 quick pulses upward from the top of the lift. Repeat on other leg.

If you are feeling strong, challenge yourself to another set of each on each side.

You can also go through the same motions while standing if you find it easier on your knees.

2. Position Butt Lifts

Lie on your back, knees bent, feet flat on the floor, and legs together. Lift hips up off the floor as high as you can and squeeze glutes at the top, then lower hips to the floor. Do this for 20 counts, then hold at the top and pulse upward in smaller quick motions for 20 counts.

Widen your feet about hip distance apart. Lift and then lower hips as before for 20 counts, then hold at the top again for 20 more pulses upward.

Widen your feet one more time to wider than hip distance apart and once again lift 20 counts and then hold up top for 20 more quick pulses upward.

If you are feeling strong, repeat the entire series again and/or place a weight on top of your hips for more of a challenge.

3. Outer Thigh Lifts

Sitting on the floor, bend one leg in front of you so that your outer calf and thigh are pressed against the floor. Rest your weight on your bent leg while stretching your other leg straight out to the oppo-site side. Keeping that top leg straight and tight, lift and lower it 100 times in ½-inch pulses. Lean your body to the opposite side if you need to. Repeat on other side with the other leg.

For a second outer thigh lift exercise, get into the same starting position as the first exercise, but instead of straightening the second leg completely, bend it at the knee, keeping your foot flexed and heel pressing back behind you. Lift knee and leg in one line, parallel to the ground, then pulse backward 100 times without letting the knee come forward past the hips. Repeat on other side.

Jené's Favorite Booty and Legs Routine

Jené's bottom-blasting weight-training routine will raise that booty and make it look good in jeans or in the buff! For maximum effectiveness, do this workout once or twice a week.

Squats

Squats are a power move that work the entire lower body, but are especially great for lean legs (by working quads and inner thighs) and building a fabulous-looking booty (and who doesn't want that?). Squats can be done using your own body weight for resistance, holding on to small dumbbells (3 to 5 pounds, or more) or a kettlebell. Or use a squat rack with a barbell held either in front of your shoulders or on your back (please consult a professional if you are unsure of your form!).

Stand with feet hip width apart, with or without weights, toes pointing slightly outward to align with the direction the knee is bending. Then sit back with your back flat and booty protruded as if trying to lower into a chair. Lower legs and butt to a 90-degree angle, then push through your heels back to a standing position while squeezing your inner thighs. Be sure knees stay firm; don't let them roll inward or go forward over your toes.

If you're looking to really target your glutes and inner thighs, try a squat with a wider stance. For this variation, also referred to as a Sumo Squat, stand with feet wider than shoulder width apart and turn toes out even more.

Please note: Form is *very important* for squats; you can hurt your knees and back if you don't do them properly. Listen to your body! If anything is hurting you during this exercise, stop immediately and check your form.

Aim to do three sets of 15 to 20 repetitions, or less if you are using heavy weights.

Walking Lunges

These work the quads, which help support the knees and create nice toned upper thighs! Keeping your back straight and shoulders back and down, step forward into a lunge with front leg bent, making sure your knees do not go past your toes; your back leg should be stretched behind you with bent knee just above the floor. Bring your back foot

forward to meet your other foot, then continue that same foot forward into another lunge, making sure to squeeze your glutes at the top. Continue to alternate legs for a count of 10 on each.

These can be done with or without weights. Try holding dumbbells in each hand, down at your sides.

Do three sets, or 60 counts total, 30 on each leg.

Stiff-Legged Dead Lifts

These work hamstrings, which are important to keeping the butt lifted, firm, and tight! Stand with feet hip distance apart, legs straight without locking knees. Hold dumbbells down in front of your thighs and bend forward, back straight and arms following the line of your legs, during a count of 3, toward your feet. Go down as far as you can in this position, hold for a second, then, using your legs and *not your back*, return to standing during another slow count of 3, and squeeze your glutes at the top.

Try to do three sets of 15!

Please note: Just as with squats, dead lifts are an exercise that you can potentially hurt yourself doing if you don't perform them properly. Form is important!

Calf Raises

Find a step or something else that gives you a little lift to get full range of motion. You may also want a wall, railing, or something else to hold on to.

Stand on the step with feet hip distance apart, heels off the step, toes pointing forward. Keeping your body upright, slowly lower heels until you feel a stretch in your calves, then slowly raise to your tippy toes. Lift and lower 20 to 30 times, depending on your level of strength. Then turn toes so they are pointing inward and repeat the up-and-down movement 20 to 30 times. Turn toes to point outward and again raise and lower 20 to 30 times.

If you don't have a step, you can also do these flat on the floor—just don't lower before lifting. You can also add weights for more resistance.

Pump It Up!

Get pumped up with a pair of pumps! Did you know wearing high heels can help tone muscles in the legs and pelvic floor? High heels change your center of gravity, causing you to activate those muscles in order to stay balanced.

"The higher your energy level, the more efficient your body. The more efficient your body, the better you feel and the more you will use your talent to produce outstanding results."

—Anthony Robbins

"Our hair is a statement of style, an affirmation of beauty,
an expression of self-love."

—Adémola Mandella

CHAPTER 6

Get Beautiful Hair!

We all want healthy, beautiful, shiny, perfectly styled hair—but for most busy girls it's a never-ending battle to get there. We complain our hair is too thin, too thick, too frizzy, too dry, too flat, doesn't hold a curl, won't grow, and the list goes on. We don't always have the time or know how to deal with our hair, so we tend to mismanage it on a regular basis and it most often gets tossed up in a ponytail or messy bun, or hidden in a hat and forgotten about.

We all should really be more aware of our hair. After all, hair is more than an adornment for our heads. It's also a statement of our health, our hygiene, our personality, and our personal style. So you have to ask yourself, what does your hair say about you?

The message of this chapter is not about having perfectly styled hair at all times, but about striving for the healthiest hair possible, which, incidentally, will always look good and save you time. We would like to help you get the healthiest hair that *your* hair can be. You will start to see amazing results as your hair continues to grow.

How does having healthy hair save you time? Well, the healthier your hair is, the less time and product you will have to use trying to make it *appear* healthy and presentable. Healthy hair is always "in."

There are many simple mistakes people make when it comes to caring for their hair, and there are many simple solutions for correcting them. We are here to help your hair to reach its greatest potential.

Hair 101

The first step on the path to healthy hair is education on the structure of your hair and its functions. Here's a quick primer of what you need to know about your hair.

What Is Keratin?

Ninety percent of your hair is made up of a protein called *keratin*, which is also found in your nails and skin. The protein in your hair determines the hair's strength, structure, and ability to maintain color.

We Always Hear Terms Like "Hair Shaft" and "Cuticle," but What Are They?

The *cuticle* is the outermost layer of the hair shaft. It forms the protective barrier for the hair

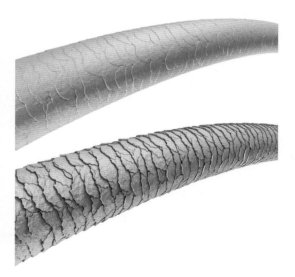

to protect the cortex (the middle layer of the hair, which gives it qualities like texture and color). The cuticle layers are thin, flat, colorless overlapping keratin scales. Magnified, they resemble the overlapping bark of a tree. When the cuticle scales are lying flat and tight, the hair is healthy and looks shiny because the light easily reflects off it.

When the cuticle layer gets damaged, the scales get roughed up and lifted, leaving the hair open and unprotected. The cuticle becomes porous (permeable), which means the hair's ability to retain moisture is lost because the moisture is escaping through the open cuticles.

What Causes Dry, Damaged Hair?

Damaged hair is dry, brittle, porous, and weak. It becomes very hard to manage and style. It affects your overall look and takes up more of your time trying to manage it. Here are some of the causes of damaged hair:

- inadequate oil production/essential fatty acids to lubricate hair

- improper diet

- improper use of hair care products for your hair type and condition

- protein/moisture imbalance in your hair

- harsh shampoos, conditioners, and hair products with a pH of over 5.5

- overwashing

- exposure to hot water, hard water, chlorine, salt water, and sun-activated hair-lightening products

- not getting regular trims every six to eight weeks

- vigorous towel drying

- excessive brushing or brushing of wet hair

- poor choice of hair tools and/or overuse of heated hair tools

- excessive heat styling

- excessive use of styling products containing alcohol

- exaggerated back-combing (maybe it's just a Jersey thing)

- environmental damage (UV rays from the sun, extreme heat and cold, wind, etc.)

- continually overprocessing the hair with repeated chemical services

- elastic bands and other hair accessories

Hair Health Tip

Hair stretches up to 50 percent when it's wet, and that is when it is the most vulnerable. *Always* use a wide-toothed comb or pick, never a brush, when detangling wet hair. Never rush through a comb-out or let the hair snap. Gently start combing on the ends of your hair and then work your way up and around your hair.

Is Your Hair Damaged?

Does Your Hair Lack Elasticity and Strength?

Hair elasticity is determined by how much the hair stretches and recovers without breaking. It should be able to stretch about 20 percent of its length when dry and about 50 percent when wet.

To test your hair's elasticity and strength, take out a piece of hair from your scalp where it is most exposed to the elements. See if the hair can stretch and return to its normal state without breaking.

If your hair breaks easily, stretches then snaps, or if, when wet, upon stretching, it feels overly soft, mushy, stretchy, spongy, or gummy and doesn't return to normal size, then you have low elasticity in your hair and a protein/moisture imbalance you need to correct.

The fix: You need a good protein/moisture balance. You should use a water-based moisturizer and do a good deep conditioning or protein treatment on your hair at least once a week, biweekly, or once a month, depending on the level of damage.

Does Your Hair Have Breakage?

Hair is weak if it breaks easily when combing or brushing. You can sometimes hear the hair snapping as it's breaking.

The fix: Use a leave-in conditioner. You may also want to use a lightweight oil on the hair to coat the strands and give them strength. Never stretch the hair when it's wet by vigorously brushing. Don't overbrush dry hair, especially if you have a lot of product in it. Try finger-styling instead of using a brush, especially if your hair is curly. Don't sleep with your hair in a tight ponytail or use rubber bands or hairbands with metal plates on them that can rip and tear the hair, causing further breakage. Use seamless coated elastic bands instead and don't wrap them around the hair too tightly. Don't overuse heated hair tools.

Is Your Hair Porous (Lacking Moisture)?

Porous hair has lost its ability to retain moisture because its cuticles are damaged and open. You can tell if your hair is porous if it dries fast, your color fades fast, hair breaks easily and feels straw-like. Porous hair can also easily absorb chemicals, as in hair color, perms, or relaxers, which can cause the hair to become overprocessed, weak, and severely damaged. As easily as hair color is absorbed, the color can also escape more easily through the open cuticles, which will cause your hair color to fade faster.

The fix: Give your hair a rest from chemical treatments! Try a keratin treatment to seal the cuticles of the hair to trap the moisture in. Give yourself weekly deep conditioning treatments and hair masks. Use a leave-in conditioner. Use a lightweight oil on the hair to coat strands and seal in moisture. Color your hair a deeper color that has bigger molecules; they won't escape the hair as easily and will help give it strength. Stay away from chlorine!

Does Your Hair Look Dull?

If your hair is dull, it's likely the cuticle is damaged and the scales are lifted, so light can't reflect off it the same way as if the cuticles were lying flat.

The fix: Wash hair less often to allow natural oils to coat the hair strands. Try getting a keratin hair treatment. Do some hot oil treatments on the hair! Dry your hair straight so that your cuticles lie flat and tight so light is able to reflect off them or use a flat iron with a heat serum to add shine. Mist lightly with a shine spray. Brighten it up with a new hair color or glaze.

Does Your Hair Look and Feel Dry/Brittle?

Hair can feel and look like straw because oil glands in the scalp are not producing or supplying enough oil to lube the strands and seal in moisture. Your scalp may be dry, itchy, and flaky. You may even have dandruff (dry flakes on the skin and scalp caused by the accumulation of oils and skin cells that block the pores).

The fix: Scalp treatments. Hot oil treatments. Protection of your hair from the UV rays of the sun or other environmental factors. Take a break from chemical processing.

Do You Have a Lot of Split Ends?

When hair is dry and brittle, the ends split.

The fix: Cut your hair! Even if it is only ⅛ of an inch every six to eight weeks just to nip the split ends off. There is no way to repair a split hair once it's been split. Apply a light oil to the ends of your hair by rubbing it first into your palms to warm it up and then gently working it through the ends of the hair to temporarily seal them.

Does Your Hair Seem Limp?

Limp hair seems to lack body, fullness, and volume or is unable to hold a curl. This can also be the result of overuse of hair products or using products that are too heavy for your hair type. Your hair is hard to style and goes flat.

The fix: Make sure you are completely rinsing out your shampoo and conditioner. Try using a clarifying shampoo to remove any existing buildup of residue on your hair from styling products or chemical services. Use lighter hair care products such as mousses or lightweight gels. Use a diffuser while uplifting the base of your hair or let your hair air-dry. Adding a few highlights can help make hair appear fuller.

Does Your Hair Tangle Easily?

Damaged cuticles can lift and get snagged on each other, which causes the hair to tangle.

The fix: When your hair starts to get easily tangled, it's giving you a clue that it's time for a haircut, as well as some deep conditioning and anti-humectant treatments to help give your hair back its strength and luster. Also, try sleeping on a satin pillowcase.

Do You Have Flyaway Hair?

Damaged hair carries a negative electrostatic charge, so the negatively charged hair strands repel each other like the force of two magnets. The hair sticks up and becomes unmanageable and frizzy.

The fix: Never rub your hair dry with a towel! Use a heat protectant spray. Use a leave-in conditioner. Apply a silicone-based hair serum or lightweight oil. Don't overbrush your hair! Use a wide-toothed comb or finger-style the hair. Apply a lightweight hairspray to fine or medium hair, or a light pomade to thicker hair. On-the-go quick fix: Use an unscented dryer sheet or a dab of lip balm. (Just a dab will do ya! Rub a little bit between your hands to warm it up, then apply to flyaway hair. It's small, compact, fits in your purse and does the job.) Look for anti-frizz labeled products on the market.

Did You Answer "Yes" to Most of These Questions?

If so, your hair is damaged. But don't despair! Your hair will continue to grow and you can use this section to learn what causes the damage, how to prevent it, and how to treat your hair going forward. A little shift in how you are caring for your hair may be the quick fix you need to change the look and health of your hair. It's never too late!

What Is Your Hair Type?

Oprah's hair stylist and author of *Andre Talks Hair!*, Andre Walker, created a broad-spectrum hair typing system that helps you to determine your hair type.

Your hair type will be a combination of one of the numbers and one of the letters.

Type 1

Hair is always straight with no curl pattern at all. It tends to be oilier than other types, which gives it a shiny appearance, but that is also because when the hair is straight, the light reflects off it easier. It is the most resilient type of hair. It may need to be washed more regularly.

Type 2

Hair has a slight wave to it and is somewhere between straight and curly. It can be resistant to styling and has a tendency to frizz.

Type 3

Hair is curly with a tendency to frizz and is damage prone.

Type 4

Hair is extremely curly to kinky. It is usually fine and fragile, so it breaks easily. It needs daily added moisture and delicate treatment. It is the driest of hair types.

Type A

Is used to describe thin and fine hair, meaning the hair has a smaller diameter. It is the most fragile. It usually has a looser wave pattern.

Type B

Is used to describe medium-textured hair and more of an S-shaped curl.

Type C

Is used to describe thick, coarse hair with a tighter, smaller curl pattern.

You can have a number of combinations of hair types:

2A wavy, fine/thin

2B wavy, medium-textured

2C wavy, thick, and coarse

3A loose curl, fine/thin

3B medium to tight curl, medium-textured

3C kinky hair in corkscrews, thick and coarse

4A kinky Afro, tightly coiled, fine/thin

4B kinky "Z" pattern, cotton-like feel, medium-textured

Is Your Hair Normal, Oily, Dry, or Combination?

If you are using too much product or the wrong products for your hair type and condition, you could be sabotaging the health and potential of your hair. Whether your hair is dry, oily, or combination, the key is in stabilizing and maintaining the moisture/protein balance in the hair.

To determine your hair type, wash your hair, then the next day (before you wash your hair again), rub a tissue on your scalp.

- an oily blot on the tissue = normal/combination hair

- nothing on the tissue = dry hair

- hair strands that are stuck together due to the oil buildup = oily hair

Normal Hair

This is the ideal hair type. Your hair is neither oily nor dry. You have a good balance between protein and moisture content in your hair. Keep in mind that you still need to maintain your healthy hair by protecting it from environmental, thermal, chemical, and mechanical appliance damage.

Dry Hair

You can go two to three days without washing your hair and without scalp or hair looking oily. Your hair looks dull, dry, lifeless, and splits and breaks easily. It becomes frizzy with dry ends when in its natural air-dried state or before you shampoo. Your scalp may feel itchy and dry. You may even see some dry flakes on the skin and scalp.

Oily Hair

If your hair is oily, you may also have oily skin. Your hair is often shiny and you consider it often looking "greasy" at times, which prompts you into washing your hair more often. In actuality, washing your hair too often will only stimulate the oil glands in your scalp into producing more oil. Try washing your hair less often.

Combination Hair

If your hair is combination, you have an oily scalp with dry ends. Ends are usually split and lighter in color than the rest of your hair.

Hair Health Tip

Do a hot oil treatment using nourishing oils such as olive oil, argan oil, avocado oil, or coconut oil two to three times weekly, or do a weekly deep conditioning treatment. It stimulates blood circulation to the scalp, which aids in hair growth and slows down hair loss, among other benefits. Warm the oil or conditioner and massage into hair and scalp, then wrap hair in a hot towel or shower cap and leave on for twenty to thirty minutes. Rinse thoroughly, then shampoo and condition as usual.

How Do You Care for Your Hair Type?

Normal Hair

Having "normal" hair is all about maintaining that protein/moisture balance! Achieve this by using a hair care regimen formulated specifically for your hair type and by paying attention to your hair's condition, so you notice and can address any issues as they develop.

Dry Hair

Caring for dry hair is all about hydrating the strands and sealing in moisture! Use a clarifying treatment regularly to remove buildup on the hair from too much protein, then give yourself a deep conditioning or hot oil treatment to add moisture and help seal it in. Use a water-based conditioner and lay off the heated appliances as much as possible. If your hair is also experiencing breakage, determine what strength protein-enriched treatment is needed, based on breakage level, to give your hair back its strength. Then follow up the treatment with a good conditioner.

Oily Hair

Don't overscrub your scalp when washing or brushing! Overscrubbing your scalp will stimulate your oil glands, which will only produce more oil. Be careful not to overcondition oily hair, because it will leave hair limp, lifeless, and oily looking. It also won't hold a curl! Apply light conditioner to the ends first, and

DIY Conditioner

In a small bowl, combine 3 tablespoons organic apple cider vinegar with 3 cups distilled water and 1 tablespoon of warm, raw, organic honey. Add any of the desired extras:

- up to 20 drops of your favorite essential oils
- 3 tablespoons of your favorite fruit oils
- herbs such as rosemary, ylang-ylang, and West Indian bay leaf to help stimulate hair growth
- a bit of natural mineral sunscreen to protect your scalp
- whole milk, rich in vitamins and minerals, to condition hair and leave it soft, silky, and shiny

Mix well, and then apply to the hair. Rinse.

then work your way up to the scalp. Do not apply directly to the scalp or hair will appear oilier. You will also benefit from using low-pH styling products on your hair. Try to avoid oily foods. It is important to eat a well-balanced diet including plenty of whole grains, omega-3s, biotin, and vitamin A.

Combination Hair

Target the area of the hair where it needs the most care and moisture. Try applying a leave-in conditioner only to the ends of the hair, where it's dry, instead of all over. There is no need to put product close to the scalp if it doesn't need it. Treat the top and the bottom of the hair as you would two separate hair types, giving each only what it needs.

Hair Health Tip

Even if you have oilier hair, try washing your hair less often. Try washing your hair (in lukewarm water, not hot!) every two days instead of every day, and always end in a cold-water rinse to "close" the cuticle. Sometimes washing your hair too often will actually cause your scalp to produce even more oil to try to replenish it. Try using a dry shampoo at the roots (usually in a spray or powder form) on the in-between days instead.

How to Tackle Thinning Tresses

Many women find themselves with thinning hair after childbirth and others just have it naturally. As we age, our hair follicles decrease in size and our hair naturally thins.

Here are some simple solutions:

- Take biotin supplements, found at any drugstore. (Check with your doctor before trying any new supplements.)

- Try washing your hair less and using water that's not too hot.

- Brush your hair and scalp with a natural bristle brush before every shampoo unless you are about to get a chemical service or your scalp is irritated. It increases blood flow to the scalp, which nourishes the roots.

- Get scalp massages as often as you can—ideally, at least once a week! Your local salon likely offers them. The massage increases blood flow to the scalp, which nourishes the roots and promotes healthy hair growth.

Help with Hair Care Products

Look for Low-pH Products and Avoid Hair Care Products That Contain Bad Chemicals

Avoid chlorine, DEA (diethanolamine), MEA (monoethanolamine), TEA (triethanolamine), FD&C color pigments, fragrances, imidazolidinyl urea, DMDM hydantoin, isopropyl alcohol, mineral oil and petrolatum, PEG, propylene glycol (PG), sodium lauryl sulfate (SLS), and sodium laureth sulfate (SLES).

Many hair gels, root lifters, volumizers, holds, and hairsprays contain these, and these ingredients

Hair Health Tip

Aloe is not just for sunburns! Put aloe vera juice (which can be found at most mass-market stores) in a spray bottle and mist it over your hair. This is a natural way to help to balance pH and help close the cuticle to remove frizz.

are carcinogenic, synthetic, and drying; they contain formaldehyde, coat your hair, or strip hair of natural moisture. Some are even active components in antifreeze!

If your shampoo lathers easily, it's a good sign that those bubbles are saying you have a shampoo with a high pH. Those harsh lathering agents can leave your hair dry and brittle.

Look for Products That Cater to Your Hair Type and Condition

Most hair care products will tell you what hair type they are for, right on the bottle, so it takes the guesswork out.

Know Your Conditioners

There's more to conditioning your hair than your daily post-shampoo conditioner use. You can also try:

RINSE-OUT DEEP CONDITIONERS

These contain humectants, emollients, or other conditioning agents that help retain moisture and are good for more intense treatment and repair. Do these treatments two to three times a week.

LEAVE-IN CONDITIONERS

These are lightweight creams or lotions that can be applied to the specific areas where you need extra moisture and protection from the environment. Don't overuse the product. Too much product will only weigh down your hair or make it look oily. Use the amount necessary according to your hair length. A shorter hairstyle may only need a pea-sized amount, but longer hair may require a little more. Warm it up in your hands and first apply to

Shine On!

A hair glaze between cuts and colors can help seal the hair color in the cuticles and give shine to dull hair. This is something you can ask your stylist for.

the bottom of the hair strands, where hair tends to be more dry, and work your way up. Never apply directly on the scalp. That will make the hair heavy and lifeless. (The ends of your hair have been around a lot longer than the hair near your scalp and most likely need the most conditioning anyway!)

SPRAY-ON DETANGLING CONDITIONERS

These are leave-in sprays that you apply while hair is wet to help smooth the cuticle and prevent tangling.

PROTEIN-ENRICHED CONDITIONERS

You may see protein-enriched products on the market that say "protein treatment" or "keratin treatment" on the label. These should be used about once a month in conjunction with your regular conditioner to add nutrients back into the hair and to help balance the proteins and oils, which add strength and resiliency. You need to have a good protein/moisture balance in your hair. Too much of either causes damage and breakage to the hair. These protein treatments come in the form of reconstructors, protein packs, deep-penetrating treatments, and light protein

treatments. Moisturize your hair after a protein treatment if the hair still feels hard and dry.

Avoid Overusing Anti-Frizz Serums/Shine Enhancers

These reduce frizz and add shine by coating the hair with mineral oils or silicone to make it appear healthier. It's only an illusion and can leave a waxy buildup on your hair over time. Don't use too much of these products. You will only need a pea-sized amount. Warm it up in your hand and apply from the ends of your hair and move up the hair shaft only where you need it. Avoid the scalp area, or hair may look oily and weighed down.

Hair-Drying How-To

Learning the best way to dry your hair is one of the most important things you can do for its health and may even save you a few styling steps using other hair tools, such as flat irons or other hot tools! Here are some of our top tips for drying your tresses.

- It's best to let hair dry naturally as much as possible. We know this is a hard thing to do for those who have the type of hair that dries very unruly, but it is in the best interest of your hair to try to let it air-dry once in a while to give it a rest from the abuse. Do it on a day when you will just be at home and not expecting visitors. Let it dry, then stick it up in a bun.

- If you don't have time to air-dry your hair and have the kind of hair that looks good if left to dry naturally, blow-dry your hair until it is

about 80 percent dry and then let it air-dry the rest of the way.

- *Never* hold the dryer directly on the hair when drying, or for too long in one spot. Keep the dryer at least six inches away from your hair and scalp.

- When buying a dryer, choose one with a diffuser attachment. It will help distribute the heat so it's not concentrated in one spot, causing more damage to the hair.

- A cool-shot button or the coolest setting on your hair dryer is great to use on your hair for a minute or two once your hair is completely dry to seal the hair cuticle for shine, smooth the hair out, and set it in place.

- There are many products on the market that help protect your hair from heat styling. Do your research. Before using heated appliances, apply a heat protection product. Using a leave-in conditioner also helps to protect and condition your hair.

- Always dry from the base of the hair at your scalp and aim the dryer toward your ends. Never blow-dry up the hair shaft, forcing the

Hair Health Tip

One of the biggest mistakes people make when blow-drying their hair for a straight, sleek style is not drying each hair section completely through before moving on to the next section. If the hair is not dried all the way through, and preferably set with a cool blast of air, the bonds of the hair will weaken and the hair will not be able to retain its shape. Instead, the hair may frizz or kink back up.

cuticles open. When the cuticles are lying flat and tight, you will have more shine to your hair!

Three Easy Steps to a Do-It-Yourself Blow-Dry!

If you are spending a lot of time and money driving to and from the hair salon just to get your hair blown out, then you may want to consider learning how to do your own blowouts. Besides saving your money, you will be able to use your time to accomplish other things.

STEP 1

Divide the front section of the hair—from the tip of one ear over the top of the head to the tip of the other ear—from the back hair section. You will dry the front section first to control difficult bangs or frizzy baby hairs around the face because they tend to dry faster. If you prefer to dry the underneath first, you can mist the top section of the hair to dampen it before drying and smoothing (making sure not to wet what you have already dried).

STEP 2

Lightly twist the hair sections that you are not drying up into a loose bun and clip with duckbill clips to keep the wet and dry hair separated. Depending on the thickness of your hair, split the back of your hair into two to four sections.

Hair Health Tip

If you like to sleep with your hair up in a loose bun or ponytail, toss the elastic hair ties; they cause pulling and breakage as you shift in your sleep. Instead, cut the top off a knee-length panty hose and loosely wrap that around your hair like a scrunchie.

Barrel Size Matters

The bigger the barrel of your brush, the more volume and less curl you'll get. Bigger barrels are better suited for longer hair. If you have shorter hair, or you have long hair and want more of a curl, use a smaller barrel.

Same goes for curling irons! And make sure the ends of your hair are always secured within the curling iron's clip before you start rolling it up, or else you'll end up with that dreaded kink at the ends.

Thinner hair: Divide the back of the hair horizontally into two sections, starting from the top of one ear, going across the top of your occipital bone, to the other ear. (You can use a rattail comb or your thumbs to divide the hair.)

Thicker hair: Divide the back of the hair with a vertical part, then split the sections in half with a horizontal part right above the ears toward your occipital bone.

Divide into even smaller sections if you have extra-curly hair.

STEP 3

Grab a two-inch section of hair from the bottom section nearest the scalp, use a brush to pull hair taut, and move dryer downward over the brush toward the ends of the hair. Keeping the hair taut as you dry it will give it a sleek, polished look.

Work your way around the scalp from the bottom up, drying each section until all sections are completely dry before moving on to the next section. Repeat with the rest of your hair.

Choosing Your Best "Do"

If you're like us, you've tried it all. Together we have gone through a spectrum of highlighted blondes to different shades of brown, black, red, and even combinations of the aforementioned. We've gone from long hair to short hair, tried bobs, and done bangs and no bangs. We've had pretty much every style short of the pixie. We understand the desire for change.

Before choosing a hairstyle, answer these questions:

- Can your hair type and condition carry the style?

- Will the style work with your wave pattern?

- Will it fit the shape and profile of your face?

- Is the hairstyle flattering with the length and shape of your nose? (*Tip:* Off-center parts take attention away from the nose.)

- Will the style work with glasses, if you wear them? (*Tip:* Have your stylist cut any bangs *while* you're wearing your glasses so you can see where your hair falls.)

- Is the style compatible with your lifestyle? (A layered style that has to be blown out every day will require a lot more maintenance than, for example, ponytail-length hair or a basic bob.)

- Will the style be easy for you to maintain?

- Is the style proportionate to your body type?

- Does it reflect your individual style?

Facial Recognition

Knowing your basic face shape will come in handy when choosing the most flattering hairstyle. How well do you know yours?

DISCOVER YOUR FACE SHAPE

Look in the mirror with your hair pulled back and away from your face. Take a lipstick and trace on the mirror the outline of your face, following your hairline, in front of your ears, jawline, and on to the bottom of your chin. At this point the shape of your face should be very clear. Now divide your face into these three zones to see your proportions.

1. forehead to eyebrows

2. eyebrows to end of nose

3. end of nose to bottom of chin

Use this information to discover your best hairstyle!

"A woman who cuts her hair is about to change her life."

—Coco Chanel

BASIC FACIAL SHAPES AND HAIRSTYLES TO FLATTER

YOUR FACE SHAPE	YOUR BEST HAIRSTYLE
Oval The forehead and jaw-line are the same width, or if the forehead has a slightly rounded hairline, it is slightly wider than the chin. 	Most hairstyles look good on an oval face; it's considered the ideal face shape because it is proportionately balanced in all facial zones. Off-the-face styles are very flattering. *Avoid:* Wearing a hairstyle that's too long, making your face appear longer.
Round Round hairline and chin; a full, wide face. 	Pick a style that creates height or volume on top of the head and closeness at the sides to create the illusion of an oval face. Layers, off-center parts, or high, sideswept bangs are good choices. Try to keep shorter styles longer than the chin to create the illusion of length in the face. Hair slightly darker at the sides than the top can make face appear longer. *Avoid:* Volume on the sides of the head, rounded bobs at chin length, straight-across blunt bangs, and hair slicked back off face.

YOUR FACE SHAPE	YOUR BEST HAIRSTYLE
Square Broad, square hairline, narrow at the middle zone of the face, and a square, strong jawline. 	Bring the shape close to the sides of the head while adding volume on top. Create waves and roundness with layers, wispy bangs, or an off-center part to soften the corners around the hairline and jaw. *Avoid:* Long hair, straight bangs, center part, hairstyle ending at the jawline (it will only accentuate the jawline more), long bob with heavy bangs, or angled cuts.
Diamond Balanced shape with a narrow forehead and chin and very wide cheekbones. The widest part of the face is at the cheekbones. 	Bring the shape close to the cheekbones and increase width at forehead and jawline. Can wear short, medium, or long hair. Shorter styles look better with fullness in the nape area to balance high cheekbones and narrow chin. Full, rounded styles and graduated bobs look good. *Avoid:* Pulling hair completely off the face, leaving the forehead completely exposed, or having no hair on the nape of the neck. Don't choose styles that lift away from the cheeks, as it creates more width in that area.

YOUR FACE SHAPE	YOUR BEST HAIRSTYLE
Triangular/Pear Narrow forehead with a wide jaw and chin. 	Go for a style that adds width to the forehead. Keep height on top and volume at the temples, tapering at the jaw. Short hair and lots of layers are good. An off-center part is best. If you have long hair, pull it back and give it some height at the top. Choose a soft fringe. Highlights at the temple area can create the illusion of width. *Avoid:* Center parts, longer hair with fullness at jaw, or flipped-out hair that adds width.
Heart-Shaped (Inverted Triangle) Face is widest at the hairline and tapers to a narrow chin. A widow's peak gives it a heart shape. 	Style hair close to the top of the head and direct it over the sides of the forehead, while adding width to the lower part of the face and nape area. This will help decrease the appearance of width at the forehead and will increase width at the jawline and chin area. A wispy or side-swept bang is a good choice. Soft, curly, chin-length hairstyles like a bob are best. Go for an off-center part. *Avoid:* Short, full hairstyles. Don't slick back or add height to the crown.

YOUR FACE SHAPE	YOUR BEST HAIRSTYLE

Oblong

Long narrow face, high forehead with hollow cheeks and a narrow chin. The area just above the cheekbones and the forehead are about the same width.

Keep hair close to the head on top, and up and away from the temples to add volume on the sides. This will make the face appear shorter and wider. Layers and waves or curls add softness and volume. Short to medium lengths above the shoulders with off-center or diagonal parts are best. Go for wispy bangs and highlights near your eyes to create the illusion of width.

Avoid: Longer styles that drag face down, making it appear longer; center parts, straight hair.

Jazz Up Your Basic Ponytail

Pump It Up!

We do love a good ponytail! And it doesn't always have to look "undone." After you put your hair in a ponytail, take a small section of hair—about ½ inch—from the bottom of the pony-tail and wrap it around the rubber band. Then secure it with a bobby pin that's the same color as your hair. Rub a small amount of hair pomade or gel on your hands and use it to smooth any flyaways on the top of your head. Voilà—a polished ponytail in minutes! You can even braid the piece of hair you are going to wrap around.

"The right hairstyle can make a plain woman beautiful and a beautiful woman unforgettable."

—Sophia Loren

"There is nothing nicer than a girl who looks happy and comfortable in her own skin."

—Peter Andre

CHAPTER 7

Get Flawless Skin!

Now that we've covered the basics of achieving shiny, healthy, beautiful hair, let's talk about our skin! Granted, we're not dermatologists, but one of us *is* a licensed cosmetologist. A cosmetologist is a beauty professional who is trained in hair, skin, and nails, including makeup. We also must mention that we've both been fortunate enough to have access to some of the top dermatologists in the country, and we've done our research thoroughly so that we can help you truly love—and care for—the skin you're in!

The skin, in case you didn't know, is the largest organ of the human body. So you must take good care of it and protect it. How we treat our skin is a reflection of how we treat ourselves. The skin is the foundation of beauty because not only does the overall health of your body shine through it, but also healthy skin will fight off signs of aging. If you help it to heal, your skin will be less susceptible to disease, infection, scarring, and injury.

Healthy skin is the base that, when prepped properly, allows makeup to go on more smoothly and effortlessly. If you have good skin, you will have fewer imperfections to correct and cover up with makeup. And luckily, taking good care of your skin does not mean skin care has to take up a lot of your time!

Get to Know Your Skin

The skin consists of a thin outer layer called the epidermis, a thicker middle layer called the dermis, and the deepest layer called the subcutaneous layer or hypodermis.

The Epidermis

This layer is very thin and consists of a protective layer of skin cells that continually shed to make way for new cells. This process is known as cell turnover. Cell turnover slows down as we age, so we need to help it along by finding ways to stimulate and speed up the production of collagen in the dermis.

Keratin is a fibrous protein found in the epidermis. The dry skin scales that you see sometimes

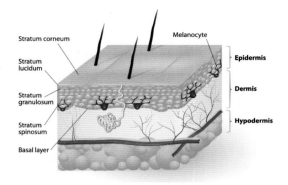

flaking off the skin are flattened cells that are actually hardened keratin.

Melanin is a substance found in the epidermal layer. It contains pigment granules called melanocytes, which give the skin its color. (It also gives hair and the iris of the eye their color.) The amount of melanin you have is a hereditary trait.

Melanin is your body's natural sunscreen, protecting you from exposure to the ultraviolet (UV) rays of the sun. The naturally darker the skin, the more protection you have from UV rays, premature aging, and skin cancer. However, even with dark skin, you still need to use a sun protectant every day.

The Dermis

The layer of skin below the epidermis that is made up of collagen, the dermis is the layer in which oil is produced. Collagen is a form of protein fiber made up of amino acids that gives the skin its strength, structural support, and durability. It's like the mesh that holds our cells together. Together, collagen and oil give our skin the support, elasticity, suppleness, and shine it needs to stay smooth, plump, youthful, and healthy.

Collagen production slows down with age, and it's the breakdown of that collagen that causes sagging in the skin and the formation of wrinkles. UV exposure, smoking, and pollution also cause collagen breakdown.

You can prevent collagen loss by taking the following measures:

- Use a sunscreen every day.

- Increase antioxidant intake (to stop the effects of free radicals).

- Eat foods and use skin-care products that contain vitamin C. (Vitamin C helps the body produce collagen, and without it amino acids can't be linked to form protein.) On skin-care labels, vitamin C is usually listed as L-ascorbic acid, ascorbyl palmitate, or ascorbyl phosphate.

- Use collagen supplements and/or creams.

- Quit smoking!

- Exfoliate! Body scrubs, loofahs, and gentle exfoliants remove the top dead layer of skin and will help speed up the natural process of skin and collagen renewal by making way for more healthy cells to rise. Chemical exfoliants such as glycolic acid and lactic acid work a little deeper into the skin.

- Use creams that contain retinoid or retinol, as it can speed up your skin's ability to turn over old skin cells and produce new skin cells.

- Try prescription-strength creams containing tretinoin, which are effective for deeper wrinkles or stretch marks.

- Look for products that contain ingredients such as copper peptides or other peptides (telomeres).

- Massage the skin daily to help boost the production of collagen to give the skin a more plump appearance and help stimulate the lymph glands to promote clear skin.

- Eat healthy food sources that promote collagen production, such as berries, citrus fruit, fish, oysters, bright red and orange vegetables, dark leafy greens, white tea, and sulfur-rich foods.

- Eat foods rich in alpha hydroxy acids, also known as AHAs, and hyaluronic acid. (These are found in many skin-care products as well!)

- Eat foods with the essential amino acid called threonine, such as lentils, peanuts, eggs, pork, beef, and chicken.

The Subcutaneous Layer

The tissue in this layer contains fat cells, which insulate the body. As we age, the cells in this layer become smaller and contribute to sagging and wrinkling. Most treatments we will be discussing do not reach this layer, so we will not be focusing on this layer in this book.

The Skin's Main Functions

- protection from the environment, injuries, and bacterial invasion

- sensation, which comes from sensory nerve fibers in the skin that send messages to the brain

Don't Be So Callused

Skin is thinnest on the eyelids and thickest on the palms and on the soles of the feet. When there is continuous pressure on one area of the skin, a callus is formed. It is just layers of hard, thickened, compacted dead skin cells.

To remove calluses (most commonly found on the feet) you can:

1. Soak feet for 20 to 30 minutes in warm water with Epsom salts or 3 tablespoons of baking soda, and add a cup of apple cider vinegar. This will soften calluses, draw out toxins, and remove the dead skin.

2. Scrub using a pumice stone.

3. Rinse feet thoroughly.

4. Dry feet and add cornstarch directly to them or sprinkle cornstarch in your socks or shoes to keep the area dry and protected.

- heat regulation

- excretion, by manufacturing perspiration (sweat), which also helps to cool the body when it's hot

- secretion, by producing sebum (oil), which lubricates and softens the skin

- absorption of moisture (which can be in the form of products applied to the skin)

- healing; as a living organ it is constantly repairing tears and injuries

- immunity, by acting as a barrier from organisms (such as bacteria and viruses) that touch or try to enter it

Healthy Skin

The health and condition of your skin reflects your diet and overall health. If you want a healthy-looking, hydrated, glowing complexion and younger-looking skin, make sure you are eating a healthy, well-balanced diet and drinking adequate amounts of water. Without it your skin may become dull, dry, and scaly, lose elasticity and firmness, or break down.

Healthy skin is:

- slightly moist

- soft

- flexible and elastic

- free from any disease or disorder

- smooth, with fine-grained texture

- resistant and self-repairing

Find Your Skin Type and Condition

Knowing your skin type and condition is crucial if you want to care for your skin properly and choose the right products for you. With the right routine and products, you'll have that youthful, healthy, glowing skin you desire.

Our best advice is to go see a skin-care consultant, dermatologist, or cosmetic surgeon who can professionally analyze your skin, diagnose a condition, prescribe a treatment plan or procedure, and determine your skin type so that you can take the guessing out of it. But we've also included a breakdown for you here so you can start getting to know your skin.

Your skin type characteristics can be influenced by:

- genetics

- nutritional deficiencies (You are what you eat! Refer back to chapter 4) and overall health and lifestyle

- seasonal changes

- hormones (from pregnancy, PMS, and menopause)

- the environment

- emotions

- the amount of secretions (oils) your sebaceous glands produce (this determines whether your skin is dry, normal, oily, or a combination)

The main goal of skin care is always to try to balance and maintain the skin's pH—with proper cleansing, exfoliation, toning, moisturizing, and hydration—as well as slow down the aging process, correct problem areas, and protect skin from the environment.

There are five basic skin types:

1. normal

2. dry

3. oily

4. combination

5. sensitive

Some argue that there are only really three basic skin types (normal, dry, and oily) instead of five. Combination and sensitive skin are sometimes considered a condition or reaction to what you are using on your skin.

Normal

This skin type is neither too oily nor too dry and shows no signs of aging, sun damage, or any other skin conditions. It is plump, soft, smooth, naturally moisturized, has no blemishes or blackheads, has even pores and skin tone, and functions well. This skin type usually burns first, and then tans.

GOAL

To maintain skin balance.

TREATMENTS

Cleanse: Use a mild daily cleanser that is pH-balanced at an acidic pH of 5.4.

Exfoliate: Use a gentle exfoliant.

Tone: Use an alcohol-free toner.

Apply serum: Use a hydrating serum. Look for serums containing A, C, and E vitamins.

Moisturize: Look for nourishing creams with properties that balance and maintain oil production and moisture to give skin exactly what it needs to continue to thrive.

Protect: Use a sunscreen daily, year-round. Look for sunscreens containing zinc oxide and titanium dioxide of SPF 30 or higher. See "The Skinny on Sunscreen" (page 119) for more information.

Dry

Dry skin appears delicate, thin, flaky, scaly, dull, papery, and even sun damaged. It can feel tight, taut, itchy, rough, dry, and uncomfortable to the touch or when making facial expressions. It has fine pores, is prone to premature aging such as fine lines and wrinkles, has few to no breakouts, and can be extremely sensitive to the sun, wind, and the cold. This skin type lacks in natural oils, fatty acids, and water.

People often confuse dry and dehydrated skin. There *is* a difference. Dry skin is a skin type that is deficient in oil. Dehydrated skin is a skin condition in which skin is deficient in water. Dehydration is usually a symptom of oily skin but can make skin *appear* dry at times. But remember: Dry skin lacks oil, whereas dehydrated skin lacks water.

GOAL

To balance the skin's water and oil by increasing moisture and hydration in the skin, softening the texture, and protecting it from the sun and environment.

TREATMENTS

Cleanse: Wash with warm water (never hot) and mild cleansing lotions formulated for dry skin. Use a rich, creamy, soothing, moisturizing, mild cleansing lotion or sulfate-free cleansing gels. Look for cleansers that contain glycerin and hyaluronic acid. Argan stem cells plump skin where there is dehydration and lack of oil. Avoid using bar soap or harsh foaming cleansers that dry out the skin.

Exfoliate: Use a gentle exfoliant to remove surface flakiness and promote cell renewal. Exfoliation will also increase the natural production of oils, which will act as a protective barrier on the skin from the environment. Don't overexfoliate by scrubbing too hard.

Tone: Use a non-alcohol-based balancing toner made with humectant ingredients to hold the moisture in the skin. Water-based toners with rose water or chamomile are beneficial to tone, restore, and hydrate the skin.

Apply serums: Apply a specialized serum and/or mask to seal in the moisture or use natural oils like sweet almond oil, argan oil, avocado oil, coconut oil, jojoba oil, olive oil, or sunflower seed oil, which are all key ingredients in dry skin treatments.

Moisturize: Dry skin benefits from water-in-oil emulsions such as heavier creams, as opposed to oil-in-water emulsions such as lotions. Use moisturizers containing protectants and emollients for a protective layer that prevents moisture loss. Choose moisturizers with ceramides, hyaluronic acid, shea butter, vitamin E, sweet beeswax, squalene, and the oils mentioned above in the serums step.

Protect: Use a sunscreen daily, year-round. Look for sunscreens containing zinc oxide and titanium dioxide of SPF 30 or higher. See "The Skinny on Sunscreen" (page 119) for more information.

Use masks: Hot oil masks are great for this skin type.

Humidify: Use a humidifier to keep moisture in the air and in your skin.

Oily

This skin type produces too much oil (secretes too much sebum). The pores appear enlarged, and skin appears sallow, greasy, shiny, and thick. The skin becomes shiny shortly after washing.

Oily skin is dehydrated skin, which means it is lacking water. Dehydration may be caused by your genetics, the natural aging process, or environmental exposure due to living in harsh climates with exposure to excess sun and wind. Your skin may be dehydrated due to lack of water from strenuous exercise, medications you are taking, too much salt in your diet, not drinking enough water, being in air-conditioned rooms for long periods of time, having poor skin hygiene, or not using the right products for your skin type. Dehydrated skin needs help retaining moisture. You need to rehydrate the cells by drinking plenty of water; eating more water-rich vegetables; taking warm (as opposed to hot) showers; avoiding harsh, stripping foaming cleansers and bar soaps; not overexfoliating; adding serums and moisturizers while the skin is still damp to seal in moisture; limiting caffeine and alcohol intake; and stopping smoking if that's a habit.

Oily skin will attract dirt and pollutants from the environment to its surface. When the pores are clogged with oil and dead skin cells, mixed with debris from the environment, this increases the thickness and coarseness of the skin, and the blocked pores result in breakouts.

Blackheads—or open comedones as they are known medically—are hardened oxidized masses of sebum mixed with dead skin cells that block the pores of the follicles, turning dark when they are exposed to the air. The black color of blackheads is *not* from dirt, nor does dirt cause them! Closed comedones—commonly known as whiteheads—are raised bumps on the skin where skin cells and sebum become trapped inside the hair follicle under the surface of the skin; because there is no opening in the surface from which the sebum can drain, bacteria begins to grow. Both blackheads and whiteheads are most commonly found in the T-zone area of the face, but can also be found just about anywhere on the face and body.

GOAL

To balance the skin by controlling the excess oil, without overtreating it, overscrubbing, or overdrying it. You need to hydrate the skin to balance the oil-and-water ratio in the skin. Use proper products to unclog the pores and kill bacteria on your skin.

TREATMENTS

Cleanse: Use a gel-based, mild foaming cleanser or gentle non-foaming cleanser containing surfactants (molecules that dissolve oil-based materials on the skin).

How Can I Make My Pores Smaller?

Unfortunately, there is no way to shrink the pores once they have become enlarged, but you can keep the pores clean and refine the skin to make the pores *appear* smaller. There are products out there with a silicone base that will sit on top of the skin and help fill in and blur pores and fine lines to give the illusion of a smooth and flawless complexion. Using a retinol-based product (a derivative of vitamin A and a well-known acne fighter and anti-ager) can make pores appear smaller.

Wash with warm to hot water to open the pores. You want to clean the skin without stripping it.

Exfoliate: Use gentle exfoliation to prevent buildup of dead skin cells, which block the pores and cause breakouts. Overexfoliating and scrubbing too hard will only aggravate the skin and activate the oil glands to produce more oil, which makes the condition worse, so don't overdo it.

Tone: Immediately after cleansing and exfoliating, apply a hydrating, alcohol-free

Leave Whiteheads Alone

You *never* want to pick a whitehead. It will only inflame the lesion, spread bacteria that can cause more breakouts, and increase the possibility of leaving a scar.

toner that won't dry out the skin, in order to remove residue, soothe and tone the skin, and balance the oil and water in oily areas. You may also use witch hazel or a salicylic acid toner. The salicylic acid will help clean out the pores and keep them clean to prevent breakouts.

Apply serum: Apply a specialized serum to protect the skin and seal in the moisture. Look for serums containing vitamins A, C, and E.

Moisturize: Make sure you use an oil-free hydrating moisturizer to help balance the skin. Hydrate the skin using a water-based moisturizer that contains humectants, which will attract water. Anti-aging products are good for this skin type as well. Look for products with hyaluronic acid to help hydrate and plump up your skin. Lotions are better to use than heavy creams in oily areas.

Protect: Use an oil-free sunscreen daily, year-round. Look for sunscreens containing zinc oxide and titanium dioxide of SPF 30 or higher. See "The Skinny on Sunscreen" (page 119) for more information.

Use masks and specialty products: Use water-based hydration masks (as opposed to oil-based) to balance out the overproduction of oil. Clay masks are great to absorb extra oils in the T-zone. Don't overuse acne products. If used improperly, they will irritate and dry out your skin, which will only activate your oil glands to produce even more oil to counteract the dryness. Try to keep a good water/oil balance in the skin.

Shine Patrol

Get some oil-blotting sheets! These can control shine during the day so that you are not constantly caking on your makeup to cover it up, which only makes the skin look worse.

Combination Skin

This skin type is a little controversial. Some would say there is no such thing as combination skin, and that if you are oily in the T-zone area, then you have oily skin. Some would argue that the dehydrated skin on the cheeks is only a symptom of inflammation in the skin, where oil buildup mixed with skin cells and debris is blocking the pores. Some would say that once you treat the skin as a whole, as an oily skin type, from the inside out and down to a cellular level, the skin will eventually balance itself out. Nevertheless, we will refer to combination skin as a skin type in this book because it is commonly considered to be one.

If you have this skin type, you have occasional breakouts, mostly in the T-zone (the area across the forehead and down the nose, including the chin), where the skin may produce more oil because it has a higher number of sebaceous glands. The pores may be slightly larger in this area as well. You see the oily shine at times in the T-zone, but on the cheeks, skin can appear dry, flaky, or scaly. Sometimes your skin changes with the seasons, making it oilier in the summer and drier or more dehydrated in the winter.

GOAL

Balance the amount of oil and moisture in the skin by addressing each area differently and properly treating its specific needs.

TREATMENTS

Combination skin-care products usually contain less oil and more water to help with dehydration and to balance the skin, similar to oily skin care. Specialized products and masks can be used to treat each area differently. The trick is to treat the oily T-zone, or problem areas, separately from the dehydrated areas, with skin care that is appropriate for each area. Certain areas of the skin may have underlying skin conditions, such as acne, that you may need to treat differently than other areas because they require a little extra treatment.

For the oily/dehydrated skin areas, see oily skin-care treatments above. For problematic skin, see "Find Your Skin Type and Condition" (page 104).

Sensitive Skin

This skin type is also controversial. Some would say that sensitive skin is not a skin type at all, but rather a condition where your skin reacts to specific triggers and stimuli and becomes irritated because it is not healthy and is unbalanced at a cellular level. *Any* skin type can have an allergic reaction. However, in this book, we will refer to sensitive skin as a skin type because it is commonly referred to that way and we have come up with solutions that may help get your sensitive skin under control.

Sensitive skin may react sensitively due to conditions such as rosacea, eczema, contact dermatitis, and acne. Sensitive skin is not the same as skin that has an allergic reaction to specific substances. If you have a reaction to products or ingredients that comes and goes, then your sensitive skin is not a permanent issue. If you have consistently recurring, problematic skin issues, then it is most likely a chronic skin condition.

Sensitive skin is delicate and thin looking, often has a smooth appearance with small pores, and looks red or flushes easily. It usually feels irritated, dry, and itchy; can be painful or uncomfortable to touch; and also gets breakouts easily. Skin care and skin treatments, along with environmental conditions such as sun, wind, and cold weather, can easily aggravate sensitive skin.

Sensitivity Test

If ever in doubt about whether or not you are sensitive to a product, do a patch test first, before you apply the product anywhere else! You do this by putting a small amount of product on the inside of the bend of the elbow where the skin is thin and waiting twenty-four hours to see if the skin there becomes irritated. If the skin is raised, inflamed, red, and/or itchy, you most likely are sensitive to the product. (Calamine lotion can help take that redness away.)

GOAL

Treat sensitive skin very gently, never use harsh ingredients on it, and avoid the sun. You are better off using all-natural, organic, mild products with minimal ingredients (the fewer the better) that are free from harsh ingredients. Look for fragrance-free and hypoallergenic cleansers, toners, moisturizers, and makeup. Look for emollients and ointments that create a barrier on the skin to seal in the moisture and protect it from the environment. Keep yourself and your skin hydrated.

TREATMENTS

Cleanse: Use a very mild, gentle cleanser. Get products specifically designed and labeled for sensitive skin. The fewer ingredients your cleanser has, the better. Try to go organic, natural, fragrance-free, and hypoallergenic. Look for glycerin as a key ingredient, to act as a protective barrier that prevents dryness. Bisabolol is an anti-irritant and anti-inflammatory that is extracted from chamomile and will help soothe stressed, inflamed, and irritated skin. Avoid cleansing soaps with harsh ingredients such as stripping acids, alcohol, fragrances, and dyes, synthetic and artificial ingredients that can irritate the skin and cause allergic reactions, such as rashes.

Exfoliate: Avoid scrubs and exfoliation tools! Try just using a washcloth with your cleanser.

Tone: Look for fragrance-free and hypoallergenic products. Try a spritz of rose water.

Apply serum: Try serums with antioxidants like vitamins C and E, green tea, licorice, coffee berry, and B3 (they are great anti-inflammatories). Olive oil and neroli oil, which has antibacterial and antiseptic properties, are also great; or apply a product with concentrated propolis, which is a compound made by bees. It's rich in amino acids, vitamins, and bioflavonoids that reduce inflammation.

Moisturize: Look for fragrance-free and hypoallergenic products and things that contain hyaluronic acid or glycerin as key ingredients to act as a protective barrier that prevents dryness. Shea butter, which

Determine Your Skin Type with the Fitzpatrick Scale

The Fitzpatrick Scale is one method for determining your skin type. It works by measuring and labeling your skin's tolerance to the sun's UVB rays (the burning rays). This method was developed by Dr. Thomas B. Fitzpatrick, a renowned Harvard dermatologist. Dermatologists and plastic surgeons refer to this scale prior to performing any aggressive peels or light therapies, laser resurfacing, plastic and corrective surgery, laser hair removal, and varicose vein injections to determine treatment selection, tolerance level, healing time, and end results. Here are the different types:

Type I: pale white; blond or red hair; blue eyes; freckles—always burns, never tans

Type II: white; fair; blond or red hair; blue, green, or hazel eyes—usually burns, tans minimally

Type III: cream white; fair with any hair or eye color; quite common—sometimes mild burn, tans uniformly

Type IV: moderate brown; typical Mediterranean skin tone—rarely burns, always tans well

Type V: dark brown; Middle Eastern skin tone—very rarely burns, tans very easily

Type VI: deeply pigmented dark brown to black—never burns, tans very easily

is an African healing remedy, and products that contain 100 percent raw manuka honey help sooth, heal, and reduce inflammation. Look for soothing and calming ingredients like chamomile, azulene oil, allantoin, lavender, camphor, calamine, rosemary, thyme, rose water, aloe vera, and lactic acids and peptides.

Protect: Sensitive skin should use a physical sunscreen rather than a chemical one. You also might want to try using Moringa oil, which is full of antioxidants and protects, feeds, and rebuilds sensitive skin while acting as a natural sunscreen.

Dealing with Acne

Acne is one of the more common skin conditions we're asked about. Here we'll help you get those blemishes under control!

20 Ways to Prevent Acne Breakouts

1. Wash face with a mild cleanser (foaming cleansers are good) at least twice a day. Use one specifically made for acne-prone skin.

2. Use a smaller-grain exfoliant because it is gentler on the skin. Don't overscrub!

3. Give the skin a rest from makeup when you don't need to be wearing it.

4. Change applicators and clean your makeup brushes often with a mild cleanser or baby shampoo. Bacteria and oils can build up on them and transfer to your face.

5. Wash your pillowcase often (about twice a week). Try not to wear hair products to bed (unless you wear a sleeping cap) because the mixture of your hair care products and your facial oils can cause breakouts. Wash your pillowcase with a mild detergent with few to no irritating ingredients like fragrance, and skip the fabric softeners. They can also irritate the skin.

6. Do not pick a blemish if it is red or has a whitehead! Picking causes infection, permanent enlargement of the pores, and scarring. It will only lead to more breakouts because the bacteria and the germs from your fingers can enter through your broken skin. It is okay to extract a blackhead if done properly. Apply alcohol to it to reduce the chance of infection.

7. Avoid touching your skin as much as possible. Wash your hands with an antibacterial soap often or at least before touching your face.

8. Clean your phone often, as well as any other devices that touch your face. The buildup of makeup and pollutants in the air mixed with oils from your face on the phone can block pores and cause breakouts. We like to use those little individually wrapped rubbing alcohol wipes you can get at the drugstore.

9. Use oil-blotting sheets throughout the day to absorb the excess oil when your skin gets shiny instead of reapplying your makeup. This will prevent your makeup from getting too cakey looking and settling in your pores.

10. Vitamins applied topically as well as internally can help improve your complexion and are essential for healthy skin. Vitamins A, B, C, and E are great for your skin.

11. A healthy diet tends to give you healthy skin.

12. Use a sunscreen especially made for the face with an SPF of 30 or higher every day, even in the winter. Try a tinted moisturizer with SPF or one that contains antioxidants like green tea, coffee berry, and vitamins A or C.

13. Use foundation or concealer on the face only where you need it. It is not necessary to cover the entire face, as it can clog pores. (Make sure you blend the foundation in, though.)

14. Toners can dry out the skin if used too often. If this happens, the skin will produce more oil to replace the oil that's lost, which will

only cause more breakouts. Toners are meant to even out the pH of the skin. Use a toner specifically made for oily skin.

15. Remember that even oily skin needs a hydration moisturizer. Find one specifically made for oily skin.

16. Don't overuse acne cream. It can irritate the skin, dry it out too much, cause redness and peeling, and increase the skin's sensitivity to the sun.

17. Exercise! It helps to rid the body of toxins. Sweat itself does not cause acne. Just make sure to wash your face after a workout because you don't want that buildup of oils on your face, which can attract particles floating around the environment that will block your pores and cause breakouts.

18. Keep your stress levels low. Stress is not only bad for your skin, but it also affects your entire body in a negative way. People seem to pick at their face when they are stressed. Breathe in deeply and out slowly to calm yourself down and reduce stress. Focus on your breath only and rid yourself of some of those toxins when you exhale.

19. Take or eat probiotics! Probiotics are the good bacteria that help your body digest food and stay balanced. They improve your immune system and your body's elimination of waste. Yogurt contains naturally occurring probiotics, or you can take a supplement. Probiotics are good for your skin and your overall health. You can even wash your face or make a mask with a plain probiotic yogurt. Add some brown sugar in the yogurt to use as a face scrub and exfoliate.

20. Get or give yourself regular facials if you are able to, to help keep the oil and water balanced in your skin.

Active Ingredients to Prevent Breakouts

When looking for products to treat acne, check the label or ask your dermatologist to prescribe a treatment with these ingredients.

- *Azelaic acid:* This is a doctor-prescribed natural medicine available as a cream or gel that kills bacteria, reduces acne inflammation, and normalizes the skin. It can help clear and prevent acne caused by bacteria and prevent new breakouts. Azelaic works well for mild to moderate outbreaks of acne.

- *Benzoyl peroxide:* This acne medicine comes in different strengths ranging from 2.5 percent to 10 percent benzoyl peroxide in lotions, gels, soaps, and liquids. It kills the bacteria that cause acne to form. However, overuse of this product will overdry and irritate the skin. Less is more, so try to just lightly spot-treat affected areas. (For a natural acne bacteria killer, try green tea.)

- *Beta hydroxy acid (BHA):* This dissolves excess oil buildup within the pores. It tends to be less irritating than alpha hydroxy acids (AHAs). Salicylic acid is a commonly used BHA in acne treatment products and chemical peel treatments. It unclogs pores and is good at exfoliating dead skin cells; however, it doesn't penetrate deep enough into the skin to fight the acne-forming bacteria as the two treatments mentioned above do. (Strawberries are naturally high in salicylic acid.)

- *Glycolic acid:* Rejuvenates the skin! Derived from sugarcane, the most common and safest form of glycolic acid is called alpha hydroxy acid, also known as AHA. It is a chemical exfoliant that is water-soluble. It will help to renew the skin, giving you a smoother and more radiant complexion after only a few applications. Using an AHA cleanser will quickly exfoliate the skin by removing dead surface layers of the skin, which will help clear and unclog the pores and reduce pimples from forming while making way for new plump skin cells to rise to the top.

  You want to use an AHA with at least 10 percent strength, which is sold over the counter. Trained cosmetologists can use AHA products that have a concentration of 20 percent to 30 percent. Dermatologists and doctors can use up to 50 to 70 percent strength on your skin.

  The most popular at-home peel is the glycolic acid peel. The higher the AHA concentration used in a chemical peel, the stronger it is on the skin and the more skin irritation, redness, and peeling it may cause.

- *Lactic acid:* Also an AHA, this ingredient will not only help exfoliate the skin, but it also acts as a humectant to help hydrate the skin. Use a cream or lotion that has less than 10 percent strength. This is great for dehydrated skin as well.

- *Stabilized vitamin C:* This is a great antioxidant to protect against free radical damage and hyperpigmentation. Bonus: It is also collagen building!

- *Sulfur:* Dries out the sebum that clogs the pores! It also promotes circulation and reduces inflammation in the skin.

Other Common Skin Concerns

Aside from acne, there are a few other major skin concerns: sun and environmental damage, premature aging, and eye area concerns. Luckily, there are a number of ways to treat these concerns!

Sun and Environmental Damage

This can appear as dehydration, which is caused by being exposed to dry, hot, cold, or windy climates and UV rays. You need to lubricate and protect your skin by creating a barrier between it and the environment. Use a high (30+) SPF sunscreen daily! Fractional laser and photo facials are also good for environmentally damaged skin.

Premature Aging (Fine Lines and Wrinkles)

Premature aging is caused by the sun, environmental exposure, and repetitive facial expressions. When underlying structures are damaged, skin loses its firmness; then lines, furrows, and wrinkles form on the face and neck. Use a sunscreen daily for prevention and protection and keep the skin hydrated and moisturized.

There are a lot of treatments and products out there that fight the effects of aging on skin. The following are some options to ask your dermatologist about.

BOTULINUM TOXIN TYPE A INJECTIONS

These temporarily relax muscles that cause frown lines, crow's feet, and smile lines.

- *Botox:* Botox immobilizes the muscles that cause forehead wrinkles, crow's feet, the lines between the eyebrows, and cleavage creases. It can even reduce the appearance of gummy smiles and lift the tip of a droopy nose. Effects last three to six months.

- *Dysport:* This does the job of Botox, but covers a wider area under the skin and is known to last for a longer period of time. Great for moderate to severe frown lines and the area around the eyes. Lasts up to four months.

- *Xeomin:* One of the newest Botox alternatives, Xeomin does not contain additives. (Both Botox and Dysport do.) Good for severe frown lines and the "11" between the eyes. Lasts three to six months.

HYALURONIC ACID

This is a moisturizing ingredient found naturally in our skin and is used in many moisturizers to keep skin plump, smooth, and hydrated.

RETINOL

A derivative of vitamin A, retinol promotes faster skin cell turnover. It can make your skin sensitive to the sun, so it's better to use as a treatment at night while your skin is at rest and indoors. It's important to use a sunscreen during the day to protect your delicate skin while using this product. It's great for decreasing fine lines and wrinkles.

FILLERS AND LASERS

If you have more time or money to invest in anti-aging procedures, ask your dermatologist or plastic surgeon about in-office procedures like fillers

Stealth Anti-Aging

Interested in lasers or fillers or Botox, but worried about the stigma? Don't be! As cosmetic laser surgeon Dr. William Song notes, "When it comes to the face, you may have no idea that someone has had work done, unless it was botched. With the many non-surgical options available, facial enhancements can be done in increments so that people will notice that you look great, without suspecting anything."

and laser treatments, which can fill in fine lines and wrinkles, plump up hollows under the eyes and other areas of the face, and increase collagen production in the skin to give you a more youthful appearance in just one quick visit. There's a lot out there, and your doctor can guide you on the best treatment for you!

Eye Area Concerns

The biggest complaints about eyes, aside from fine lines and wrinkles? Dark circles and puffiness.

Dark circles can have several causes. If you have fair, thin skin under the eyes thanks to genetics, they may appear no matter what you do. Allergies or poor diet can be to blame. And aging is another factor. As the skin ages, collagen production slows down and there is loss of subcutaneous fat under the skin, causing it to thin out and making the veins underneath more visible, which casts a dark shadowy hue under the eyes.

Puffy eyes, or so-called "bags" under the eyes, are due to excess fluid in the connective tissue around the eyes and stem from similar causes: genetics, aging (as subcutaneous fat shifts), allergies. But they can also be caused by colds or other infections, hormonal changes, lack of sleep, or too much salt intake.

For dark circles, fillers and laser treatments can be used to plump up the skin, adding fullness where the skin is thin and lacking volume in order to camouflage underlying veins.

Some home solutions for both issues? Prop your head up higher with an extra pillow while you sleep (and be sure to get enough rest!). A cold compress in the morning can also help. Keep two spoons in the freezer (or try cold tea bags or cucumber slices) and hold under the eyes for about five minutes, or try gently dabbing on an eye cream daily (no rubbing!), preferably one with caffeine or one that's retinol- or hyaluronic acid–based to stimulate circulation and help to constrict blood vessels.

Aging Skin by Age

Triple board-certified plastic surgeon Dr. Ramtin Kassir provided this rundown of what to watch out for by decade:

In your 20s: signs of sun damage

In your 30s: sun damage, wrinkles, and some volume loss

In your 40s: more volume loss and wrinkling

In your 50s: sag at the neck and jowls

How to Do a Weekly At-Home Facial

Facials treat, correct, and protect the skin. It is important to know your skin type and condition so you can choose the facial products that will most benefit your skin. When facials are done regularly and properly, you will see a very noticeable improvement in skin tone, texture, and appearance. Pay attention to the areas of the face that need special help. Learn to recognize various skin conditions so you know how to treat the problem

area and when you should see a dermatologist for treatment.

A preservative facial treatment should be applied to maintain the health of the skin. It cleanses your skin properly, increases circulation, relaxes the nerves, and activates the skin glands and metabolism through massage.

A corrective facial treatment should be applied to correct skin conditions such as dryness, aging lines, oiliness, blackheads, and other minor conditions of acne.

Facial Benefits

- deeply cleanses the skin

- exfoliates

- increases blood and lymph circulation, which helps to remove impurities

- activates glandular activity

- tones and relaxes skin

- helps correct skin conditions and disorders with specific treatments

- prevents premature aging of the skin, such as fine lines and wrinkles

- protects the skin

- relaxes the nerves

- maintains muscle tone if massaged in the right direction

- strengthens weak muscle tissue

- softens and improves skin tone, texture, and complexion

- gives you more confidence, since your skin will look glowing and healthy

Facial Tools

These are available at most beauty supply stores, convenience stores, or supermarket beauty sections.

- headband or clip to hold your hair back off your face

- sanitized facial sponges or disposable 4" x 4" cotton pads

- 2" x 2" round cotton eye pads (alternatively, use a couple of cucumber slices)

- spatulas or cotton swabs, for removing product from its container or excess eye makeup

- 2 mask brushes (alternatively, if you are going to be using your hands to apply the mask, make sure to wash and sanitize them appropriately by using an antibacterial soap before touching your face)

- gauze (for mask); optional

- circular palette or condiment cups

- gloves, if you want to protect your hands from product

- astringent

- skin-care products for your specific needs (cleanser, exfoliant, toner, mask, corrective serums, moisturizer, sunscreen)

- facial steamer, or bowl with hot water and towel to hold over head for trapping steam and opening pores

Facial Steps

Did you know a proper facial is a twelve-step process? Because Jacqueline is a licensed cosmetologist, we can let you in on this important beauty regime secret straight from her professional skin-care training!

1. Analyze your skin. Know your skin type and condition.

2. Select products according to your skin type and condition to meet your specific needs.

3. Wash your hands with an antibacterial hand soap.

4. Remove makeup, starting with the eyes and lips.

5. Cleanse the face.

6. Exfoliate.

7. Tone.

8. Apply specialized serums, boosters, and corrective treatments.

9. Apply mask.

10. Tone.

11. Moisturize.

12. Protect (use a sunscreen with SPF 30 or higher).

As much as that regime is an ideal beauty habit to stick with, not all busy girls can make the time for all those steps. When low on time, make sure you at least cleanse, tone, moisturize, and protect.

The best thing to do to cut your beauty regime down a few steps and still have your skin receive all the great benefits is to use multifunctional products with specialized benefits. New hybrid skin-care products merge hydrating, anti-aging, brightening, and protection for the skin into one product.

At night, when you are tired and don't want to put your energy into skin care, just use a makeup

The 3-Step Morning Rush Routine

If you're short on time in the morning but still want to treat your skin well, just stick with these three steps:

1. Cleanse with a mild cleanser.

2. Tone the skin.

3. Moisturize and protect with sunscreen.

remover facial cleansing cloth with multiple purposes (that you can even keep on your nightstand) to remove makeup, tone, and hydrate the skin, then apply a sleep mask. This is a great way to give your skin what it needs while it's at rest, without spending a lot of time or layering on multiple products.

The Skinny on Sunscreen

We can't express enough how important it is to apply a sunscreen to your face *daily*. Sunscreen protects your skin from harmful UV rays that can damage the genetic structure of the cells and sometimes lead to cancer. UV rays can also cause premature aging of the skin such as wrinkling, sunspots, and loss of elasticity, which causes sagging and hyperpigmentation.

Remember that it is just as important to wear sunscreen in the winter as it is in the summer, even on cloudy days, to protect your skin against incidental exposure. Be mindful that the sun's harmful rays can penetrate through the windshield of your car. You may even want to wear sunscreen or gloves on your hands to protect them from age spots and wrinkling while you're driving. The time

you spend in the sun running in and out of a store adds up for incidental exposure time too!

Use a sunscreen with an SPF of 30 or more. There are also specific sunscreens designed for the eye area. You need a sunscreen with both UVA/UVB protection. Be aware that there are no products on the market as of now that block 100 percent of the UV rays, but FDA-approved zinc oxide and titanium dioxide minerals are the best choices. Sunscreens with these ingredients are called physical sunscreens. Physical sunscreens reflect the rays away from the skin before they can damage the skin.

Waterproof or water-resistant formulas are also a good choice. Try to avoid sunscreens with ingredients such as oxybenzone, aka Parsol 1789 (although this is FDA approved), retinyl palmitate, or retinol. Sunscreens with these ingredients are called chemical sunscreens. Chemical sunscreens act as a sponge that absorbs the harmful UVA and UVB rays and converts them into infrared heat.

If you don't like doing the extra step of applying a sunscreen, then find a moisturizer that contains one. There are also some really good SPF tinted moisturizers on the market, or you could opt for a BB or CC cream, both of which provide more coverage than tinted moisturizers but less than foundation, along with added skin benefits like antioxidants and, in CC cream's case, "color correctors" that make your skin look radiant.

Finally, on days when you're in the sun a lot, wear a hat and sunglasses for additional protection.

Now that your skin is beautifully prepped and ready to go . . . let's *get made up!*

"Beauty is about enhancing what you have.
Let yourself shine through."

—Janelle Monáe

CHAPTER 8

Get Made Up!

We're guilty of it, and we're sure you are too. Running out the door with just a ponytail and a dab of ChapStick. While we all know we have natural beauty, and that's to be appreciated, sometimes just going that extra step can make us feel even better about ourselves and ready to face the world! But, we don't mean lacquering on heavy foundations or a ton of eye makeup. It's all about finding a few key cosmetic products and techniques that work for you, accentuate your best facial features, and fit into your busy life.

The first thing you need to know about getting made up before you decide that it's too overwhelming and intimidating to try is that makeup *really* doesn't have to be difficult or even time consuming to apply. Although creating and displaying can be a glorious form of art for the artistically inclined makeup enthusiast, it can also be simple, fun, quick, and natural, even for a no-fuss kind of girl. We will break it down and make it easy for you. Just take it one step at a time. Getting made up is about discovering new ways to enhance and awaken the beauty that already exists within you.

Skin Prep: Creating the Perfect Canvas

Before applying any makeup, it is extremely important to prep your skin if you want to achieve the best and most flattering results. Create a clean canvas by making sure your skin is washed, exfoliated, and moisturized.

1. Remove existing makeup.

2. Cleanse.

3. Exfoliate.

4. Tone.

5. Apply serum.

6. Apply an eye cream.

7. Apply moisturizer.

8. Apply sunblock.

9. Apply lip balm and/or primer to exfoliated lips.

Primers

Apply a face primer or pore minimizer before applying your foundation to reduce the appearance of pores and help the foundation to glide on smoothly and evenly for a longer wear.

Apply an eye shadow base primer to make your eye shadow appear more vibrant, prevent it from creasing, and allow it to stay on longer. There are even waterproof formulas available. Choose a nude or color base, whichever you prefer. (We prefer nude.) Using your ring finger, tap product onto eyelid and blend across the eyelid and up toward the brow.

Apply a lip primer to prepare the lips for color; smooth their texture; make your lipstick, liner, and gloss color more vibrant; allow your lipstick to stay on longer; and prevent your lip liner from feathering.

DIY Lip Exfoliant

Mix coconut oil with brown sugar and apply to lips. Using a toothbrush, brush your lips in a circular motion to exfoliate and soften dry lips.

Apply eyebrow and eyelash serums, growth enhancers, and primers as instructed in the next sections in this chapter.

Beauty Tools: The 5 Must-Have Brushes

Having these brushes handy will make makeup application much easier!

1. *Eyebrow brush:* Two-for-one tool for filling in brows with the angled brush on one end, and applying color and blending with the spooly end.

2. *Foundation stippling brush:* Flat shape with rounded edges. This flame-shaped brush can blend a lot better than your fingers, especially when it comes to crevices like below your eyes and around your nose.

3. *Kabuki brush:* This short, wide brush with a flat base (no handle) is great for distributing powder or bronzer on the "high planes" of the face such as cheekbones, forehead, and nose for a natural glow.

How to Clean Makeup Brushes

Don't forget that makeup brushes can harbor dirt and bacteria, which can contribute to breakouts! Some professionals say to clean your makeup brushes at least once a month. We suggest you wash your dry brushes (used for powders) once every two weeks and your wet brushes (used for foundations and concealers) every week if used on a daily basis. Swirl brushes in a bowl full of a few squirts of baby shampoo and warm water. (Dr. Bronner's Tea Tree Pure-Castile Liquid Soap is also a great choice for cleaning brushes.) Push and squeeze any buildup on the brushes, starting from the base and through to the ends of the brush hairs/fibers, then rinse, pat down, and let air-dry.

4. *Blush/bronzer brush:* Medium-sized round or angled brush with soft bristles that is perfect for applying blush across the cheekbones. Use circular motions when applying to achieve a natural-looking flush to your face and to avoid looking like you applied two colored stripes.

5. *Eye shadow brush:* A small, soft brush for applying powered eye shadow to lids.

The How on Brows

In terms of your face—after healthy skin, of course—great-looking eyebrows are arguably what has the most impact on your overall look. Whether you are a high-maintenance or low-maintenance girl, the same rule still applies: *Never* neglect your brows!

Eyebrow Shaping

Eyebrow shapes and styles have changed many times over the decades. If you look back on pictures from different eras, you will see a distinctive look from each time period. Because brow styles are ever changing, you can go with the latest fad or just go with what you feel looks best on you. The first step is deciding what shape and style you want to achieve.

"The most beautiful makeup of a woman is passion. But cosmetics are easier to buy."

—Yves Saint Laurent

The Advantages of Eyebrow Grooming

- Eyebrows frame our face.
- They help to balance our facial features to make them look more proportionate.
- They can give the illusion of the eyes being closer together or farther apart.
- They can visually lift and open the eyes, drawing more attention to them.
- You can achieve your best look that will flatter your features. (Too thin and too arched an eyebrow can leave you with a constant look of surprise worse than bad Botox; too heavy an eyebrow can close the eyes and overpower the face.
- You can help the eyebrows appear fuller or extended in areas that are sparse and/or overtweezed.
- You can give your eyebrows a more defined arch.
- Eyebrows can help hide scarring and other imperfections.
- You can shape your eyebrows to leave room for more eye shadow to play and contour with.
- You can deepen or soften your look by adding color to the brows.
- Eyebrow shapes can give a more youthful appearance.

WHERE SHOULD EYEBROWS BEGIN AND END? HOW DO YOU FIND YOUR ARCH?

If you are new to properly shaping and maintaining your eyebrows, then these steps will teach you the correct way to achieve that goal. Eventually, with experience, you won't need to use the white pencil marks as a guide on where to tweeze because your judgment will get better and you will find it easier and faster to shape and maintain brows that are already well groomed.

1. Align a pencil vertically with the side of your nose and inner corner of the eye and up past the eyebrow. Any eyebrow hair that is past the inner corner of the eye should get tweezed. If you have wide-set eyes, leave the eyebrows a little closer together to give the illusion of the eyes being closer together. If you have close-set eyes, leave the eyebrows a little farther apart. Eyebrows normally should be about one eye distance apart from each other. Separate the areas to be tweezed

from the area you leave alone by drawing a line with a white eye pencil.

2. To find the high point of where the arch should be, while looking straight ahead, align your pencil vertically along the outside edge of the colored part of the eye (the iris). Where the pencil hits your brow is where the high point of the arch should be. Mark with a white eye pencil if needed.

3. Align the pencil diagonally along the side of the end of your nose and across the outer corner of your eye and upward through the brow. Tweeze any hair over that line unless you have close-set eyes. In that case, leave the hair extended a little longer. If you have wide-set eyes, then make the brow a little shorter. Mark with your white pencil if needed.

4. There should be a straight line from where your eyebrow starts and ends. Check the alignment by holding your pencil horizontally under the brow from its beginning point to its ending point. If the brows are uneven, either tweeze one side or draw in with a color filler to give the illusion that they are even.

BROW RECOMMENDATIONS BY FACE SHAPE

One good way to determine how to shape your brows is by looking at your face shape. Although we feel that there are no rules when it comes to the creativity of brow shapes these days, these face shapes can be used as a guide for choosing an eyebrow shape best suited to flatter you. It's all about creating balance.

FACE SHAPE	BROW SHAPE
Oval	Try a subtle, arched brow.
Round	Try a high, arched brow that can give the illusion of a more elongated face. Try to avoid a rounded brow.
Elongated	Try a flat, straight eyebrow shape that can give the illusion of shortening the face.
Diamond	Try a curved brow that can help soften the sharp angles of the face.
Square	Try a thicker, curved brow with a little arch; it can help soften the sharp angles of the face.
Heart-Shaped	A subtle, rounded eyebrow is most flattering.

Eyebrow Hair Removal Methods

There are three main methods you can use to remove eyebrow hair: tweezing, waxing, and threading.

TWEEZING

If you are one of those girls who has to go to a professional every time you need to remove some stray hairs or change the shape your eyebrows, save yourself some time and money and learn how to do it yourself! We are going to teach you a new skill . . . the art of tweezing. We promise you that after a little practice you will quickly see that it is not as difficult as you may have originally thought. We have confidence that you will master this skill before you know it. Let's get started!

Tools for Tweezing

1. mirror (magnifying mirror is best to see stray hairs that need tweezing)

2. hot washcloth to steam and soften brow

3. baby tooth-numbing gel (if desired)

4. white eyebrow pencil (to mark where you need to tweeze, if necessary)

5. tweezers (slant-tipped)

6. witch hazel or astringent

7. cotton-tipped swabs

8. eyebrow comb/brush (or clean toothbrush)

9. small scissors

10. eyebrow pencil, eyebrow color powder, or eyebrow gel

11. gel mascara (color or clear) or hairspray

Step-by-Step Tweezing How-To

1. Soften the brow area by steaming it with a hot, wet washcloth. Hold for a minute to open up the pore of the hair follicle for easier hair removal. (Don't use ice cubes or cold water for numbing. The coldness will close the pores, which will tighten around the hair follicle, making it more difficult to remove.)

2. Start tweezing in the area between the brows, making sure to hold the skin taut with the thumb and index finger. Tweeze at the base of the hair in firm, quick motions in the direction of the hair growth. Never tweeze in the opposite direction of the hair growth. Apply witch hazel or astringent

Makeup Tip

Eyebrow stencils can help you achieve a perfect eyebrow shape even if you lack experience and skill in eyebrow shaping. They come in a variety of shapes and styles.

with a moistened cotton-tipped swab to any tweezed area immediately after you finish.

3. Tweeze any stray hairs that are above the shape of the eyebrow and not connected to it! Make sure not to tweeze into the hair needed for the shape and bulk of the brow. Apply astringent.

4. Tweeze any stray hairs that you see beneath the shape you chose for your eyebrow. You may want to just follow the natural shape of your brows by tweezing out the strays. Whatever shape you choose, again, be very careful not to overtweeze into the shape of the brow. Apply astringent.

5. Take your brow brush and brush the eyebrow hair upward and, using a small scissor, trim any extended hair that goes up and over the shape of the brow.

6. Using your brow brush, brush the brow hair downward and check for any extended hair that falls below the shape of your brow and trim using your small scissor, then brush your brows back into their proper place.

WAXING

This is a common method for shaping the eyebrows and taking all the stray hairs off in one swoop instead of painstakingly plucking each individual one. At-home waxing kits are available at drugstores; however, you should be cautious, since if you don't apply and remove the wax correctly, it's easy to remove too much hair at once. You also have to remember to apply the wax in the direction of the hair growth and remove it quickly in the opposite direction while holding the area taut.

Professionals at most hair and nail salons can do waxing. Waxing really only needs to be done once a month or so and then you can follow the shape and tweeze stray hairs that grow in between waxings if you need to.

THREADING

Eyebrow threading originated in parts of India and the Middle East and Far East. It is a hair removal technique that uses 100 percent cotton thread that is doubled, twisted, and then rolled along the surface of the skin over areas of unwanted hair. It catches the hairs in the thread and then in one clean sweep quickly lifts them out of the hair follicle. If you are going to a professional for this service, just make sure you use an experienced aesthetician in threading because an inexperienced threader can cause eyebrow hair to break or look uneven, or cause ingrown hairs and/or unnecessary pain.

The Advantages of Threading

- It's quicker than tweezing because it removes more hair at once.

- It's cheaper than waxing and doesn't require a lot of tools.

- It's less messy than waxing, and also cleaner because nothing but the thread touches the skin. It is very sanitary.

- It's more precise because it removes the light peach fuzz that you normally don't pay attention to while tweezing. This gives your brows a cleaner look.

- It's 100 percent natural, so it's great for sensitive skin because no chemicals are needed.

- It's more gentle on the skin than waxing because sometimes waxing can remove skin, while threading does not.

- Frequent threading can cause the hair follicle to become damaged and eventually stop growing hair (meaning less brow maintenance).

- It does not cause ingrown hairs.

- This technique is more entertaining to watch than other hair removal methods!

Finishing the Look

After you finish grooming those brows, decide whether you are using an eyebrow pencil, eyebrow powder, or an eyebrow gel (see more information on these methods below) to color and blend into the brow to fill in any sparse areas that need to be filled in. This gives the brow a more structured shape. Using an eyebrow pencil, use light, short, quick feathered strokes to look like little hairs, and then blend using an eyebrow brush, keeping in line with the shape of the brow. If you need to extend the look of your brows, do so at this time, keeping in mind where the end points should be for the brow shape that best suits you.

Use an eyebrow gel that resembles mascara to brush and hold the eyebrow hairs in place, or use your eyebrow brush with a little hairspray spritzed on it to set the look. Clear mascara that you can get at any drugstore works great for this purpose, but watch to make sure that it is not drying too white and flaky!

Brow Tinting and Brow Fillers

There are two easy ways to go about emphasizing your brows: by tinting or by using fillers. Whichever way you decide, choose a color that is a shade lighter than your hair color and in the same tone. A lighter brow can soften and open your face. Unless your hair is blond or very pale, then choose a color that is a shade or two deeper that coordinates with your hair color. Here's what we recommend for specific hair colors:

- Blond or very pale hair: Go a shade or two deeper. Try an ash blond, taupe, or soft gray.

- Light brown hair: Going a shade or two darker will give you more definition. Try a taupe or sable.

- Red hair: Try an ash blond, auburn, or camel.

- Brunette hair: Depending on your shade level and tone, go a shade or two lighter than the hair on your head. Try a sable, warm or dark brown, or even a mahogany.

- Black hair: Darkest brown but never black. You can even use a dark gray.

- Gray hair: Slate or gray.

- White hair: Use a gray or ash blond.

TINTING

Brows can be tinted just like the hair on your head (preferably by a professional), and that will be a little longer lasting than temporarily coloring them in. But keep in mind that as your eyebrows naturally grow and shed, so will your tinted brow color.

Tinting the eyebrows even gets the light fuzzy baby hair underneath and makes the eyebrow appear thicker, so you won't need to rely on eyebrow filler such as a pencil, powder, gel, or brow pen.

FILLERS

Eyebrow Pencil

Eyebrow pencil tends to contain more wax than an eyeliner pencil, but in an emergency, you can substitute with it. Apply in short, quick, light feathery strokes, keeping in line with the brow shape. Soften the look by brushing over the penciled-in area with a brow brush or the spooly tip at the end of most eyebrow liners.

Eyebrow Powder

Gives a more natural, soft look. You can substitute with a matte eye shadow if you need to. Remember to use a stiff, flat, angled brush to apply with light strokes. Applying a clear brow gel or mascara over the powder can set the look.

Eyebrow Gel

Holds the brow hair into place. Gels come in clear or in different ranges of colors. They come in a mascara type wand or in a pot. Be careful of the clear gels that dry white and flaky looking. For the kind of gel that comes in a pot, use a stiff, flat, angled brush. Apply using quick, light strokes in the direction of the growth while moving upward and across the eyebrow, starting closest to the nose. Don't overapply. You can also use an ointment like Aquaphor, Vaseline, a petroleum jelly–based lip balm like Rosebud Salve, or even some clear mascara to keep the eyebrow hairs in place.

Eyebrow Felt-Tip Pen

Use this long-lasting pen to outline the eyebrows and fill them in with light, feather-like strokes. Mastering this technique takes practice. You don't want to overdo it or it will look too harsh. An oil-based eye makeup remover will take this product off much easier than a non-oil-based remover.

Eyebrow Extensions

Yes, that's right, there are eyebrow extension services out there now, just like for the eyelashes, to add a little fullness to your brows. This will need to be maintained every few weeks, but it's an option. We don't recommend this on oily skin or if you are living in a humid climate.

Foundation, Concealer, Blush, Bronzer, and Highlighter

How to Match Your Foundation to Your Face

A big makeup challenge for a lot of women seems to be finding the right shade of foundation—and then applying it properly! To find your perfect foundation for a flawless face, you will need to be able to identify these four things:

- the undertones in your skin (pink, yellow, or neutral, and whether your skin is light, medium, or dark)

- your skin type (as discussed in the previous chapter) to know whether you need an oil-free foundation or specific beneficial ingredients

- the desired level of coverage (sheer, light, medium, heavy) depending on what you are trying to cover

- the finish you are looking for (matte to deflect the light or dewy/creamy to attract it and give it more moisture)

Seeing a defined line where your makeup meets your face is a big no-no, as is going too dark or too light with your foundation; both can leave you looking unbalanced with the rest of your body's skin tone. Take our tips and spend some time at a variety of department store cosmetic counters to test out different foundations with different undertones until you find your match. Someone at one of the cosmetic counters should be able to help you figure it out.

We talked to the very talented celebrity makeup artist George Miguel to get his advice on picking out the right tone of foundation. He also gave us some tips for applying natural, everyday highlighting and contouring makeup.

"Treat your makeup like jewelry for the face. Play with colors, shapes, structure—it can transform you."

—François Nars

Makeup Tip

You can always mix a dab of foundation with your favorite moisturizer to make your own tinted moisturizer. It gives you a healthy, dewy glow.

GEORGE MIGUEL, CELEBRITY MAKEUP ARTIST, SAYS . . .

Foundation typically consists of three basic undertones: yellow, pink, and neutral. Everyone's natural undertones will match one of these three tones.

To match foundation to your skin, put a little foundation along your jawline to see how it blends with your natural undertone, and then you can adjust the depth of color to match your skin. Make sure it blends seamlessly into your neck.

When applying, be sure that there is no break or variation in color at your chest (décolletage), chin, or forehead. You should also blend your foundation down into your neck and even into your décolletage, if exposed, to avoid the obvious line of demarcation on your jawline.

Once your base tone is achieved, you can add some definition by contouring. An easy way to contour is to get a pressed powder that is one to two shades darker than your natural skin tone. This is also a more natural way to bronze the skin than using an actual bronzer. Use a contour or fluffy angled brush to sweep color along your temples, underneath your cheekbones, and along the bottom of your jawline going into your neck.

Applying a Blush/Bronzer

1. Apply bronzer using a bronzer brush or kabuki brush, making sure to tap off excess powder first. Apply over your makeup to contour areas of the face, such as under the cheekbones, along the sides of the nose, and on any areas where you want a sun-kissed glow.

2. Blend along cheekbones and up along your hairline.

3. Be careful not to apply the product farther in from the imaginary line that runs down from the iris of your eye down to your cheekbone (past the middle of your cheek).

Makeup Tip

As your skin changes color throughout the seasons, you can add a lighter or darker shade of another foundation to your current foundation to warm it up or cool it down.

SHADES OF BLUSH

It's best to choose a blush based on your skin tone:

Fair skin: Peaches, light coral, or apricot shades work best.

Medium/olive skin: Warm pinks, apricots, brownish rose, corals, and bronze work well.

Dark skin: Choose berry, plum, and rose shades.

Concealer

Concealer is one of our favorite cosmetics. If we were stranded on an island and could only have one product, this would probably be it . . . in close running with mascara. Concealer can camouflage dark circles, shadows, discolorations, and other imperfections to help you achieve that flawless look. But it's important to know how to choose and apply it properly.

One of the questions we always get is, "Do I put concealer on before or after my foundation?" Well, that depends on who you are asking. It's a personal preference. There is no right or wrong way, as long as you achieve your desired result in the end.

Our best answer would be, if you have a lot of corrective work to do with camouflaging discolorations, blemishes, and redness in the skin, you may want to correct those areas first with your concealer before you layer over with your foundation, and then you can always touch up again afterward if you still need a little extra help concealing. Typically, if your skin is in overall pretty good shape, you can apply your base foundation first, then correct and blend in touches of concealer where you still need coverage.

George Miguel advises: "Highlight by applying an eye concealer or an eye brightener under the eyes. It's better to use a pink undertone concealer to camouflage blue or purple undertones and a yellow-based concealer for red tones. This will neutralize the color and brighten the eye area instead of making it look gray and fatigued. One big mistake people make is selecting a concealer that is one to two shades lighter than their natural skin color, which only draws more attention to the under-eye area rather than correcting it."

HOW TO APPLY CONCEALER

1. Warm up concealer between your thumb and fingertip so it will glide on smoother.

2. Tap concealer on imperfections with ring finger to blend for a natural-looking finish. (Why the ring finger? Because the skin under the eye is very delicate and you want to avoid too much pressure on it. The ring finger is not as strong as your pointer or middle fingers, so it's gentler on the skin.) You can also use a concealer brush.

3. Apply to dark circles under the eyes, patting on the inner and outer corners, then going from each side toward the center to blend.

4. Use it in the creases around your nose and on blemishes, sunspots, and pregnancy marks.

5. You can also use it to highlight the shadows around your smile lines.

6. Use a shade or two deeper than your own skin tone to create shadows of contour on your face.

7. Try an under-eye concealer with brightening boost and light-reflecting pigments (you can also use it to highlight right under the brow). It's a great quick pick-me-up to make eyes look fresh. Using your fingertip, pat under your eyes in an outward and upward direction.

Highlighter

Use this to brighten and accentuate the high planes of your face and to revive and perk up dull-looking skin for a youthful, healthy glow. You can also mix it with your favorite body lotion to use on your décolletage as well as on other parts of your body. A subtle shimmer is divine, but you want to keep it from looking too frosty or metallic. Illuminate, shimmer, glow! Let's *go*!

Where to use highlighter:

- under the eyebrow arch (lightly and subtle, not eighties style)
- inner corners of the eyes

"Beauty is how you feel on the inside, and it reflects in your eyes."

—Sophia Loren

- middle of the eyelid
- middle of the lips over your lipstick
- just above your blush (something with a little shimmer is nice for an evening look)
- Cupid's bow (right above the top lip)
- bridge of the nose
- collarbone
- chin

Eye Shadow and Eyeliner

Basic Eye Shadow

When applying eye shadow, you can always mix and match colors and tones as you please—it's okay to get creative! But here's a guide to applying eye shadow using three basic shades.

Tip: You always want to start your eye shadow after applying an eye shadow base/primer (for the reasons given previously under the primer section) and before you apply your eyeliner and mascara.

- Use a color palette with light, medium, and dark tones.

- Start by patting a medium- to light-toned color across the entire lid to just above the eye crease.

- Apply a darker tone in a sideways "V" along the lash line and up toward the end of your eyebrow on the outer corner of the eyelid, keeping it in the crease and working it inward, about halfway across the lid. Blend well into the crease.

- Take the darker color you used for the outer "V," or a medium shade, and blend it into your bottom lash line, keeping it soft without harsh lines.

- Add a subtle highlight color under the arch of the brow to add a little brightness and to highlight. (A matte shadow is best for this area; shimmer may look a little outdated.)

- Blend the eye shadow so you don't see any harsh lines or dense color patches.

- Add a dab of light color to the middle of the eyelid to give the illusion of opening and brightening up the eye. A shimmery color is okay to use in this area.

- Add a highlighting color to the inner corner of each eye to brighten.

If you have small, close-set eyes, keep the dark colors on the outer corners of the eyes and use a light color on the inner corners of the eyes and over most of the lid. A dab of a highlighted shimmer in the middle of the eyelid will open up the eyes even more.

If you have wide-set eyes, use a darker color on the inner and outer corners of the eyes and connect it into the crease. Use a medium- to light-tone shadow in the middle of the lid. Make sure to soften the lines by blending.

THE SMOKY EYE

Smoky, sultry eyes can be done using medium to deep bronze tones, violet to dark purples/plums, and even bronze to black or dark smoky grays, to name just a few combos. You can have fun experimenting with different shades and tones. The application is basically the same for any color combination. Use a palette that has a range of shades from dark to light.

- Start with an eye shadow base/primer.

- Apply the darkest color across the eyelid, into the crease, and blend into the top and bottom lash lines, keeping in line with the outer corner of the eyebrows.

- Apply a medium color just above the crease.

- The lightest matte color goes right under the arch of the brow.

- Blend with your makeup brush to soften any harsh lines.

- Apply eyeliner, smudging it in close along the upper lash line.

- Lastly, add your mascara. If you are looking for a more dramatic effect, add false lashes.

- Make sure your eyebrows are filled in and defined to balance the look.

Flattering Eye Shadow Shades for Your Eye Color

If you happen to be familiar with the color wheel, locate your eye color on it, and try wearing color shades directly across from it on the wheel—or use the handy chart below.

Eyeliner

When applying eyeliner, our suggestion is to use a liquid pen eyeliner on your top lid closest to your lashes after you have applied your eye shadow and after you have curled your eyelashes. We suggest you then just smudge eye shadow a shade or two lighter than the liquid pen underneath the bottom lashes so it doesn't look as harsh. If you use a pencil liner underneath your eyes, make sure you smudge out the harsh line; you can even add a little shadow over it to blend it in even more.

You may also use a dark eye pencil inside the bottom inner rim of the waterline. This makes the eyes appear smaller but bolder and deeper. Adding a soft pink or pale white pencil to the inner rim can give the appearance of opening up the eyes. Using a navy blue pencil on the inner rim can make the whites of the eyes look brighter.

To achieve the winged-liner look, start by applying your liquid liner at the inner corners of the eye and drag along the lash line until you near the end of your lash line. Then turn your liner in the other direction and place it directly on the point where you decide you want your wing to end, and glide

EYE COLOR	EYE SHADOW SHADES
Blue	Golden browns, bronze, copper, terra-cotta, tangerine, peach, gray-brown, mauve, eggplant, and taupe.
Brown	Because brown is a neutral color, you can go with most colors on the spectrum. Try different shades of brown like reddish-golden browns, greenish gold, mossy greens, forest greens, blues like navy (or go bold with cobalt), charcoal, silver, or deep purples or go light with lilac, lavender, and peachy tones.
Gray	Charcoal, pearly gray, silver, navy blue, eggplant, and light purples.
Green	Browns, bronze, copper, rust, golds, purples, plums, and wine.
Hazel	Rich browns, golden-yellow browns, rust, taupe, gray, khaki, lavender, violet, plum, burgundy, and eggplant.

the liner inward to meet the liner you began with. Allow a few seconds to dry.

If you are one of those people whose eyeliner immediately ends up under your eyes, try using a waterproof formula. It will be much longer lasting for you. All waterproof makeup can be taken off very easily with an oil-based product remover.

Eyelashes

We *love* lashes! They can really make our peepers pop and add a little flirtatious playfulness to our eye batting. Enhancing your eyelashes will not only make lashes appear fuller, longer, thicker, and darker, but it will also make the eyes appear larger, wider, and brighter. Lashes give you a more alert and youthful appearance.

On the market today we have many options to help us achieve beautiful, long, full, sexy lashes, including curlers, hi-tech mascaras, tinting, conditioners and growth enhancers/serums, false eyelashes, and extensions. Here's a run-through

of what you can do to make those lashes lovely and luxurious. We'll also share some solutions for hypotrichosis (inadequate or not enough lashes).

Eyelash Curlers

These make the eyelashes look longer, curl lashes upward, and help to open up the eyes. We recommend curling your eyelashes before you apply mascara so the mascara doesn't clump together and stick to the curler, risking pulling out your eyelashes. If you use the lash curler after you apply mascara, just be careful to release it very gently so as not to rip your lashes out.

Mascara

Mascara comes in a variety of colors and formulas, and offers different wands for different purposes. There are mascaras out there that claim to lengthen, curl, lift, separate, or smudge. Choose a mascara that fits your needs and desires.

If you're unhappy with the results from the mascara you are currently using, experiment with

"For beautiful eyes, look for the good in others; for beautiful lips, speak only words of kindness; and for poise, walk with the knowledge that you are never alone."

—Audrey Hepburn

others until you reach your desired results. You don't have to spend a lot of money—there are a lot of inexpensive drugstore brands that even celeb makeup artists use and recommend. It's all trial and error.

MASCARA COLORS

First of all, black mascara works for everyone, so don't be afraid of it. The point is to accentuate your eyes with your lashes, so the darker the better. However, if you are a blond and feel black looks a bit too harsh on you, try using a black-brown, a dark brown, or another shade of brown. Feel free to have some fun experimenting with other fun and playful colors, like the blues, greens, purples, burgundies, mahoganies, etc., that are out there. There are no rules.

MASCARA FORMULAS

- *Curling mascara:* Resins and waxes in a curling mascara help to lift and bend the lashes.

- *Lengthening mascara:* Nylon fibers act as extensions to lengthen lashes.

- *Waterproof mascara:* Great for humid weather, if your eyes tend to water, or if you are looking for a longer-lasting staying power. It should not run, smudge, smear, or clump when wet. Just be careful what you use to remove it so you're not rubbing too hard or breaking lashes. Use an oil-based remover to break down the formula to remove it easily. Coconut oil works great too!

- *Cake mascara:* This type of brush-on mascara can be layered upon the lashes so you can control the depth and definition without clumping. This kind of mascara is long lasting and very sanitary because the brush applicator is separate from the formula and is washed after each use. (Make sure you use a lash comb with this formula to separate and define the lashes after application.)

- *Fiber mascara:* Has tiny threadlike microfibers made from rayon, silk, or nylon that attach to your lashes to strengthen, thicken, and add volume. They give the effect of false lashes.

- *Clear mascara:* Used for a natural look to separate the lashes and hold in place. (This can also be used to hold the brows in place.) No color and no clumps!

- *Lash gloss:* Paints on like a lip gloss and adds shine to your lashes to give you a wet, patent-leather look.

MASCARA WANDS

Different-shaped and -sized wands serve different and specific purposes. Look for mascaras that have the right combo of wand and formula to get your desired look. For example, if you want to add length and fullness to your lashes, look for a lengthening mascara formula with a thick, bushy wand that will hold more product. If you want length and separation, look for a lengthening formula with a spiky spaced-bristle brush.

Here are a few examples of the mascara wands that are out there and their purposes.

- *Comb wand:* Defines, separates, and adds length but not volume.

- *Spiky spaced-bristle wand:* Separates and defines lashes.

- *Ball-shaped brush:* For precise application to each eyelash individually. Works in smaller sections for more control separating and defining the lashes.

- *Curved wand:* Helps to lift and curl the lashes. (Use with the curve facing upward and start at the base of the lashes.)

- *Curved spheres:* Gives straight, short lashes length, volume, and curl.

- *Straight-bristle wand:* Gives natural-looking volume and length.

- *Tapered-bristle (or heart-shaped) wand:* The thicker part of the brush is great for volume and length, and the tapered tip is great for definition and coating individual lashes. It's also easy to use on the inner-corner lashes.

- *Short-bristle wand:* For short lashes like the bottom lashes.

- *Close-together bristle or bushy, thick wand:* Gives fullness/thickness to sparse lashes because the bristles grab and coat each lash, packing on more product.

- *Corkscrew-bristle wand:* A double-helix-style brush that gives volume and length to short hairs.

- *Rubber wand with spaced bristles:* For natural-looking, defined lashes without volume or length.

- *Bristle-free wand:* For added thickness at the base of the lashes.

- *Expandable-tip wand:* Controls how separated the bristles are for different looks.

Some people prefer to combine mascaras to achieve the final look they want, but some of the newest mascaras on the market already have a combination of the above bristles on each wand for applying to different areas and achieving the different looks desired.

HOW TO APPLY MASCARA

1. Apply as your last eye makeup step to avoid getting any powder from eye shadows or face makeup on the eyelashes during application.

Eyelash Primers and Sealers

You may want to add an eyelash primer before applying your mascara as a base layer, to build, lengthen, and define your eyelashes and achieve an even bigger and bolder look. Conditioning primers also help protect your lashes from breaking by keeping them healthy and strong. It is not a necessary step for daily use, as today's mascaras are formulated to do enough of the work on their own, but you can still use an eyelash primer if you want a little extra boost to your lashes. We personally prefer the tinted formulas to the white formulas.

Some brands also offer clear waterproof "top coats" to add on top of mascara to seal in the color and hold the lashes in place.

2. Don't pump the mascara wand, because it pumps air into the tube and will dry out your mascara faster and contaminate the mascara with bacteria. Instead, insert the wand into the container and twist the wand back and forth. Lift out, carefully wiping any excess mascara along the rim.

3. Working from underneath your upper lashes and holding the mascara wand horizontally, starting at the base of your lashes, wiggle the applicator wand back and forth as you move the wand up toward the tip of your lashes, pulling the mascara all the way through the ends. (It's important to start the mascara at the very base of the lashes for support, fullness, and symmetry.)

4. Give the top side of your lashes a coat of mascara as well to add some balance and strength.

5. Next, hold the wand vertically and brush the tip of your lashes quickly back and forth (like a windshield wiper), then in swift upward strokes across the length of the lashes to help separate the lashes. Also holding vertically, dab the tip of the wand into the small lashes at the inner corner of your eye for an extra eye-opening effect. Repeat until the desired result is achieved.

6. Follow the same instructions as above for the lower lashes, but brush the mascara on the top side of the lashes instead of underneath. Putting mascara on your lower lashes will open up the eyes and give a more dramatic look.

7. Use a lash comb, if needed, to separate your lashes and get rid of any unwanted clumping.

Makeup Tip

Makeup expires just like milk! Mascara has a two- to three-month shelf life. When it starts to smell or get too dry or sticky (or starts clumping), toss it!

8. Allow mascara to dry before applying a second coat.

You can soften your look by either lightly applying one coat of mascara instead of two or by using a brown mascara or no mascara at all on your bottom lashes. You may even try black mascara on the top and brown on the bottom.

Any smudged mascara left on the skin during the application process can be removed carefully with the end of a cotton swab moistened with a little eye makeup remover.

Eyelash Conditioners and Growth Enhancers/Serums

Eyelash conditioners and serums not only improve the look of your eyelashes, but also help to improve the overall health and follicles of your eyelashes.

There are some FDA-approved prescription growth enhancers on the market that promise to grow longer, thicker, stronger, fuller, darker lashes in about fourteen to sixteen weeks. However, please note that most prescription eyelash enhancer formulations include prostaglandin, a hormone that can be potentially dangerous and cause irreversible side effects such as changing the pigmentation of the iris to brown and giving you blurred vision.

There are also some non-prescription peptide eyelash conditioning systems that claim to enhance the eyelashes naturally using natural plant extracts, biotin and soy protein, and natural ingredients such as polypeptides and amino acids to help rejuvenate lashes, make them strong and protect against breakage, and make them fuller, darker, and longer. It takes about fourteen weeks of use once or twice a day, depending on the manufacturer's instructions. These are also hormone-free and paraben-free and are great for eyebrows and lower lash growth.

False Lashes

False lashes are a makeup artist's secret and can be applied at home. There are individual false lashes and strip versions as well. There are *so* many different lengths, styles, and colors of false eyelashes, so you need to choose the look you are going for. We recommend false eyelashes with an invisible strip because they look more natural. With individual lashes, you have the ability to control placement.

HOW TO APPLY STRIP LASHES OUR WAY

1. If you are applying eyeliner, do this step prior to applying your lashes, and give your lashes one light coat of mascara.

2. Gently pull each lash strip from the plastic container.

3. Hold lash strip along your lash line to measure the length of the strip to your own lash line. Trim the length of the strip lashes from the outer corners to fit the length of your lash line if needed. The eyelash strip should follow your natural eyelashes and not overhang. The lashes should also be longer toward the outer corner of the eye and shorter toward the inner corner of the eye.

4. Gently run the glue in a thin line along the inside line of the lash strip, making sure the ends are also covered. (You don't need a lot of glue to get your lashes to hold. Less is more.) You can also apply the glue to your lash strip with a toothpick.

5. Wait about ten seconds for the glue to get tacky so it adheres better.

6. While holding the lash strip at a 45-degree angle, gently apply from the inner corner of your eye to your outer corner, as close to your natural contour and lash line as possible, and then press the lash strip down, making sure both ends are attached. (Using a magnifying mirror will help you to see better.)

7. Carefully pinch the false lash to your real lash for a few seconds as the eyelash glue dries.

8. Once the glue has dried, and if you are really skilled and careful, you can use an eyelash curler to blend the false eyelashes to your real ones even more before applying your mascara.

9. Once the glue has dried, apply another coat of liquid eyeliner on top of the lash line to blend if needed, and then add a coat or two

of mascara to blend your real lashes with the false ones.

There are lash applicators you can purchase to guide your application if you can't seem to get a good grasp with your fingers. You may also use tweezers. It's easiest to apply the tiny individual lashes to your lash line with a pair of tweezers. Apply wherever you feel your lashes are sparse. You can even apply them on top of your strip lashes for a little more length and/or fullness.

CHOOSING LASH STYLE AND GLUE

Choosing a lash style is very similar to choosing mascara because the choice is based on what you are trying to achieve. Do you want longer, fuller, separated, and defined lashes? Short and full? Whatever you desire, there is a falsie option.

We personally prefer drugstore-brand false lashes and a dark-toned waterproof eyelash glue. The white eyelash glue dries clear and is much more forgiving than the dark-tone glue, but it is not as dramatic . . . and we are dramatic! If your eyes are sensitive to lash adhesive, try latex-free adhesive glue. We also like the lashes that gradually get longer on the ends for that cat-eye look.

Here are our falsie recommendations for different eye shapes:

EYE SHAPE	LASH TYPE
Almond	This eye shape generally looks good in any lashes.
Wide-set, hooded, or small	Use a lash strip where the lashes are longer in the middle, which gives the illusion of opening up the eyes. Or use full crisscross lashes to add volume and curl to lift the eyes upward and make them appear bigger and more open. For small eyes, you may want to go a little more wispy and long than full.
Close-set or deep-set	Use longer outer corner lashes to elongate the eyes.
Down-set	Use longer outer corner lashes to give the illusion of lifting and turning up the ends.
Round or large	Use a demi-lash on the outer corners to balance the eyes.

REMOVING FALSE LASHES

Ripping and pulling off your false lashes can damage or pull out your natural lashes. Instead, dip a cotton swab into some makeup remover (oil-based if you used a waterproof glue) and gently rub along your lash line to help loosen the glue. Allow the makeup remover to sit for a minute in order give it time to dissolve the glue, and then gently remove the strip. Remove the rest of your eye makeup as you normally would.

Can you reuse the lash strips? Yes! Just remove the dried eyelash glue from the lash line on the strip and reapply. You can generally get a few uses out of them. (*Tip:* They are much easier to reuse if you did not apply mascara to them.)

Lash Extensions

Lash extensions come in numerous lengths, thicknesses, and curls. Most salons offer this service, but it's important that you have a highly recommended and extremely skilled licensed aesthetician or cosmetologist apply them, otherwise you may risk damaging your natural lashes.

Lip Service

Hmm . . . lipsticks, lip stains, or lip glosses? Creamy, matte, sheer, or shimmery formulas? Hydrating, moisturizing, long wearing, shiny? Nudes, pinks, light browns, reds? Do you need a lip liner or not?

Deciding what to put on your lips can be very overwhelming. There is so much to choose from, yet so little time or—let's face it—patience. Luckily we're here to help you figure it out!

"Beauty, to me, is about being comfortable in your own skin. That, or a kick-ass red lipstick."

—Gwyneth Paltrow

What Is the Difference between Cream, Matte, Sheer, Shimmer, and Stain?

Cream (crème) lipstick: Between a matte and a gloss. These contain more wax than matte lipstick and are a little more hydrating and moisturizing. Unless heavily pigmented, they may need to be applied more often.

Matte lipstick: Deflects light and lacks shine and moisture. They contain a lot of pigment and tend to be longer lasting than other formulations, but can also be drying.

Sheer lipstick: Super creamy and moisturizing with a light feel and coverage. These are sheer with a hint of color and a shiny finish, and often contain nourishing, vitamin-rich benefits.

Shimmer: Contains light-reflecting particles. Long wearing. Makes lips pop and appear plumper!

Stain: Usually comes in liquid or gel form. It enhances your natural lip color, and is smudge-proof. It is also longer lasting than a lipstick, so, like other long-wearing color, can be drying.

Lip Liner

Lip liner not only helps define the shape of your lips, but it can also make them appear larger or smaller and prevent your lipstick from bleeding or feathering.

It's more attractive and on trend if you don't see the line of your lip liner, so make sure if you are using one that it blends into your lipstick. The days of brown lip liner with pale lips are out! Try a waterproof lip liner if your skin tends to be on the oily side or if you have trouble keeping your lipstick on. It will stay on longer.

To apply lip liner, start with primed lips. Apply your lip liner either slightly above or below your

Makeup Tip

A subtle gold shimmer looks better on warmer olive and darker skin tones, whereas a gloss with a subtle pink or silver shimmer looks better on cooler, fair skin tones.

natural lip line (depending on whether you want your lips to look larger or smaller).

Choosing a Lip Color

The first thing you want to do when choosing a lip color is figure out the undertones of your skin: Are you fair, medium (olive), or dark? Everyone usually falls between a cooler pink (fair) and a warmer yellow (medium, olive) undertone, or a more neutral combination.

Look at the veins in your hands and wrists in natural sunlight. Do your veins tend to look more green or blue? Or do you see both colors?

green veins = yellow undertones

blue veins = pink undertones

combination = neutral undertones

Dark-toned lipsticks (blue or black shades) can make your teeth look yellow, age you, and tend to look a bit severe. On the other end of the spectrum,

UNDERTONES	LIP COLORS
Yellow	Warmer colors such as peach, salmon, coral, nude, pale pinks, brownish pinks, rose, copper, or bronze *Nudes:* Sandy or caramel beiges or sheer pink *Reds:* Brick reds
Pink	Cooler colors with undertones of blue or purple, mauves, apricots, or pinks, or go bold with cranberry or fuchsia *Nudes:* Rosy beige, dusty pale pink *Reds:* Bold cherry reds
Neutral or Dark Skin	Deep plums, wine, burgundy, berries, deep reds, copper, or bronze *Nudes:* Rosy mauve or caramel rose *Reds:* Deep reds, ruby, and deep pinks with shades of purple

too pale a neutral tone can make you look sickly and unhealthy.

In finding a lipstick shade, generally, going a shade or two darker than your natural lip color will be most flattering.

For a nude lip, the best and most flattering nude lip color is slightly brighter or deeper than your skin tone. Going a shade lighter can brighten up and flatter dark-toned skin. And if you're going to line your lips, make sure you find a nude lip liner that you can blend well into your natural lips.

Makeup Tip

Stay away from trying to match your lips to your outfit (or your nails)! It's too matchy-matchy and takes away from the rest of your face.

How to Apply Lipstick and Keep It On

- Start by exfoliating your lips. (Flaky, dry lips are not flattering!)

- Line and fill in lips with a nude liner.

- Apply a lipstick primer.

- Apply lipstick from the center of your lips and then blend out, tapering carefully to the corners and making sure not to go outside the natural shape of your lips. Don't get too much in the corners of your mouth or you'll get the clown-mouth effect. (You can even just apply it to the bottom lip and rub your lips together to distribute the color to the top for a softer look.)

- Blot your lips to remove excess lipstick and allow the color to press into and stain your lips. (Or use a lip stain as a base.)

"If I had to teach someone just one thing about lip color, it would be this: Find a lipstick that looks good on your face when you are wearing absolutely no makeup."

—Bobbi Brown

- Now that you have your stain, apply a second coat of lipstick for full color distribution, shine, and overall effect.

- Adjust and define your Cupid's bow. (Some people like to draw an "X" in the center of the lip to make the Cupid's bow more defined.)

- Put your clean pointer finger between the middle of your closed lips and slowly drag it out, taking away any excess lipstick that could have eventually ended up on your teeth.

- Apply a gloss for more added shine, if desired. A lighter shade gloss can lighten and brighten up a dark lipstick.

Tips for a Fuller Upper Lip

- Dab and blend a highlight color just above the Cupid's bow to help define the upper lip.

- Apply a lip liner slightly above the natural lip line on the top lip, and blend into your lip.

- Apply lip color of your choice, keeping in mind that the darker the color, the thinner your lips will look.

- Use a highlighter shade lip color at least a level or two lighter than the lip color you're using and dab in the middle of both your upper and lower lips. Blend out slightly.

- Add a gloss with a subtle shimmer over your lip color to make both lips pop! You can even try using a matte that is a shade or two lighter.

Get Pouty! Tips for a Fuller Bottom Lip

- Use a lip pencil that is one shade darker than your lip color.

- Place liner slightly below the natural bottom lip line and blend upward into your lip with light strokes.

- Apply lip color of your choice. The lighter the color, the bigger, fuller, and plumper your lip will appear.

- Use a highlighter shade lip color at least a level or two lighter than the lip color you're using and dab in the middle of your bottom lip. Blend out slightly.

- Use a gloss with a slight shimmer over your lip color.

The 5-Minute Face

In a hurry? Here are our quick tips for getting made up in five minutes flat!

- Always start with a fresh, clean canvas by prepping your face with primer.

- Apply a hydrating light- to medium-coverage foundation or tinted moisturizer to even out your skin tone and give you a healthy glow.

- Apply an eye shadow base/primer to even out skin tone and provide a clean canvas and smooth finish.

- Apply a concealer under the eyes and over any imperfections or blemishes.

- Apply bronzer/blush for a pop of color on your cheeks and up along your temples. Lightly brush onto eyelids for a little added sun-kissed look.

- Apply eyeliner to upper lash line only.

- Curl the eyelashes and apply mascara to upper and lower lashes to open those eyes and make them pop.

- Apply a rose-tint lip balm that gives you a little color and leaves your lips soft and protected. (*Tip:* You can apply a cheek and lip stain to cover two areas with one product.)

"Nothing makes a woman more beautiful than the belief that she *is* beautiful."

—Sophia Loren

Going from Day to Evening

To go from a soft, natural day look into an evening look, all you have to do is pick a main feature on your face and amp it up!

For the eyes, use bolder colors on top of what you already have on. Go a little darker in the crease. You can also add a little shimmer or glitter shadow to the eyelid. Go a little bolder with your eyeliner, curl up those eyelashes, and add some more mascara.

If you're focusing on your lips, add a bolder color and/or some gloss or shimmer to play them up. That's really all you need!

Makeup Tip

Go with a dramatic lip or a dramatic eye, but do not do both at the same time! It looks overly made up.

"A girl should be two things: who and what she wants."

–Coco Chanel

"Style is a way to say who you are without having to speak."

—Rachel Zoe

CHAPTER 9

Get Stylish and Sexy!

Most books will tell you that you can take a quiz to figure out your "style identity." Or that you can simply achieve your own personal style by dressing like your favorite celeb. Well, we think that's bunk. You should dress like, well, *you*! And *you* might be different on a daily basis depending on your mood, the weather, or where you are in life (the "you" at twenty will certainly dress differently than the "you" at forty . . . or so we'd hope). As a TV style expert, Jené doles out advice on the regular to women of all ages, shapes, sizes, and walks of life, and the most important message remains consistent no matter what the topic: Wear what makes you feel like the best *you* you can be.

Personal style is about more than grabbing what you like on the rack, in the magazines, or on your favorite celeb. It's about dressing age appropriately, working with the figure you've got, and accommodating *your* life (for example, a stay-at-home mom shouldn't have a closet full of pumps and pencil skirts, much like a working professional shouldn't have a closet entirely full of leggings and

yoga pants). So here we share our advice on how to work with what you've got!

Dressing for Any Age

No one wants to be that middle-aged mom in the miniskirt and crop top, or that twentysomething on her first job interview in a dated pantsuit. But just because you're over sixty, it doesn't mean you have to look matronly. And if you're in your thirties or forties, stretch marks, sagging, and Spanx may be in your vernacular, but you can still rock a trend or two without looking like you're dressing "too young."

As we age, certain things happen to our bodies that we may not like and that make it harder to be more confident about the skin we're in. While it's certainly not the same for everyone (we all have that friend who still has the same figure she had when she was eighteen), there are ways we can accentuate what we like, and deemphasize what we don't. Here are some suggestions for how!

YOUR AGE	COMMON FIGURE WOES	LOOK FOR/TOSS
20s	none	(Really? Did you think we'd have any advice for you? You can wear anything! Bitches.)
30s	stretch marks, muffin top, baby weight	*Look For:* Tailored separates, well-made shoes, and a big-girl handbag! *Toss:* Low-rise jeans, rock concert shirts, anything midriff-baring worn old school (the *new* midriff-baring outfits, mostly midriff tops worn with long skirts, are more tasteful!).
40s	bra bulge, back fat, body changes	*Look For:* Dresses in classic silhouettes, investment pieces like blazers, belted trench coats, and shoes—and shapewear! *Toss:* Too-short minis, anything with graphics or prints that look juvenile.
50s and Beyond	batwings (jiggly arms), sagging	*Look For:* Well-made clothes that fit, like cardigans, jackets, slacks, and blouses; nude stacked-heel pumps with square toe box (lower heel for comfort, wider toe box for comfort, and nude to lengthen legs in a shrinking frame!); tailored trousers; pretty scarves. *Toss:* Anything too trendy, panty hose (they can look old lady-ish).

Wardrobe Essentials All Women Should Own

You don't have to have the most clothes or even the most style sense to look great. With a few simple basics, you can work with what you've got and look completely pulled together!

1. *Great bra* (more details on that below)

2. *Body shaper* (more on that below too!)

3. *Utility pair of jeans* (more on finding the perfect pair below!)

4. *Belted trench coat:* This is a super-flattering and timeless style that transcends all seasons!

5. *Nude heels:* Yes, these really do elongate the legs and go with everything.

6. *Classic black pumps:* Be sure they're scuff-free, and look for pointy toes or round

toes and thinner heels—avoid anything too clunky!

7. *Scarves:* These can jazz up any humdrum outfit with a pop of color or of-the-moment print, without spending a fortune!

8. *Belts:* Belts are a woman's best friend. They can create curves (for a straighter woman, you can use a skinny belt just below the bustline to highlight the waistline) or create that coveted hourglass shape (wider belts at the natural waist are great for balancing out curvier gals).

9. *Black blazer:* Or one in every color, really. These are timeless—just keep the shape tailored.

10. *Statement handbag:* Self-explanatory.

11. *Shades:* Sunglasses aren't just for the beach or for celebs who are hiding from the paps. They are a quick fix to looking glamorous on even your most dressed-down days. Oh, and they hide the fact that you're not wearing any makeup!

12. *Ballet flats:* Shoes are the most forgiving if you gain a few pounds, so go ahead and invest! We love a great pair of black ballet flats that go with everything, from your boyfriend jeans and blazers, to a summery sundress, to your office clothes. Choose a metallic pair as a fun neutral and alternative to black!

13. *Pencil skirt (basic black, denim, or neutral colored):* Not to be paired with aforementioned black blazer, a pencil skirt

Quick Style Tip

Outdated style rules still reign supreme, and we're here to squash them! Fashion design king Michael Kors once told Jené that it's okay to wear white after Labor Day—and we agree!

that hits just above the knee and comes up a little higher on the waist is super flattering on almost all shapes! Pair with a great print button-down blouse or a cardi with a thin T-shirt underneath. You can also keep a pair of opaque tights on hand for winter months.

14. *LBD (little black dress):* **What do you reach for when you have that wedding for that cousin of a cousin and you have no clue what to wear?** Your LBD. Or how about that office party with a conservative crowd where you still want to show off your shape? Your LBD. A "little black dress" is an essential in every woman's wardrobe for a variety of occasions.

15. *Leggings:* Just when we thought skinny jeans were our worst enemy, leggings hit the scene to show us that skinny staples didn't have to be scary. Just get a well-constructed pair in a thicker fabric that's a little more forgiving and also isn't see-through when stretched onto the body (trust us, see-through leggings happen more than you think, adding fuel to the "leggings aren't pants" debate!). Leggings also look great tucked into a tall pair of boots with an oversized sweater, button-up, etc.

16. *Fun rain boots:* Depending on where you live, you most likely need weather-appropriate footwear, and rain boots can get you through any inclement weather, including snow. We like ours tall with leg warmers peeking out for extra warmth!

17. *Crisp white button-down blouse:* Can be worn for almost all occasions, dressed up with a pencil skirt, dressed down with jeans . . . it goes with everything!

18. *Chambray shirt:* Another staple. You can mix denim-on-denim by pairing this with dark jeans under a colorful blazer.

19. *Tailored black dress pants:* These can go with anything for any occasion and they never go out of style. Be sure they fit well and are cared for properly (black pants can fade, the fabric can "ball up," and they can wrinkle, so dry-cleaning is recommended).

Quick Style Tip

Fit and tailoring are even more important than quality when it comes to clothing! You can shop the sale rack and find a great steal, and then take it to your tailor and make it look like couture. You can tailor everything from your bras to your jeans and existing wardrobe for that perfect fit!

Lorna Burford's JEAN-IUS Guide to Finding Your Perfect-Fitting Jeans

As we mentioned in our wardrobe essentials guide, denim should be a staple for all women, but most revert to leggings these days because they can never seem to find jeans that fit their shape. Use the guide below from Lorna Burford (@LornaRaindrops), denim expert of *DenimBlog* and *The Jeans Blog*, to find your pair, and then take to your tailor for a truly perfect fit!

Remember, just like bras, jeans stretch out with wear, so be sure they aren't too baggy in areas like the waist, butt, and knees when you buy them. Do the "squat test"—squat while wearing them in the dressing room, then stand back up—to see how well they retain their shape. Higher-quality denim will hold its shape and structure better than others.

Jeans for Pear and Triangular Body Shapes

If you have curves around the hip and butt, it can be harder to find jeans that balance out your proportions and are flattering rather than awkward. To really enhance your shape and give credit to your booty, look for jeans with these fits:

- *Boot cut or wider flares:* These will help balance out the hips and keep your legs in proportion.

- *Long inseams:* Having a longer length means you can wear heels under your flares and boot-cut jeans. This will elongate your legs and make them look slimmer.

- *Higher rise:* I recommend buying your jeans with a higher rise, as they are very balancing to your shape, plus they hide a multitude of sins if you suffer from muffin-top issues like so many of us do.

- *Jeans with a smaller-fitting waist:* Most ladies with wider hips struggle to find jeans that don't leave a gap at the back of their butt. I recommend trying something like Levi's Curve ID Bold Curve jeans, as they are designed specifically for your shape and are cut smaller in the waist than the hips.

- *Larger back pockets:* It's important to enhance your booty since you are blessed with it, so look for larger back pockets, as small ones can make it look bigger.

- *Stretch denim:* Always look for stretch denim—it will hug your body better, creating a more sleek silhouette.

Boots: If you do want to go for a skinny jean, I always recommend tucking them into boots, to help balance out the hips.

Jeans for Hourglass and Curvy Body Shapes

You ladies are lucky with this body shape: You can get away with most things and look great. It's all about the styling and keeping your proportions balanced. Here are some great jeans to look for:

- *Skinny jeans:* I think skinnies are the most flattering on hourglass shapes. Your chest and hips are in proportion with each other already, so showing your legs off in skinnies only highlights that point. I find that boot-cut jeans can actually overwhelm you and hide your frame.

- *Higher rise:* I recommend higher rises because the waistband will sit at the smallest part of your waist. This will also give the illusion of an even slimmer middle.

- *Medium-size back pockets:* Don't go too big or too small with your back pocket. It's important to enhance your butt, so choose wisely!

- *Skinny flares:* If you want to do flared jeans, choose a pair that is tight and skinny all the way to the knee and then has a slight flare. This is much more flattering than jeans that flare lower on the leg or have a wider flare.

- *Flares:* If you have a very curvy hourglass figure and carry a lot of weight on the hips, a flared jean will really help balance that out.

Jeans for Rounded and Apple Body Shapes

For those of you who carry your issues around your tummy area and always struggle to find jeans that are flattering or give you that shape you are looking for, there are definitely options for you too!

THE BEST POCKETS FOR YOUR BOOTY

petite/short/small bottom	small pockets
flat bottom	pockets with volume, like ones with flaps or detail
round bottom	plain, bigger, low pockets
large bottom	plain, bigger, wide, low pockets
wide bottom	vertical, close-sitting pockets

Embrace your body shape and work with it rather than against it. These are some styles to look for:

- *Skinny jeans:* Skinny jeans can look really good when they are paired with a floaty, gypsy-style top, as this will hide your problem area but the skinnies will still be fitted, creating a balanced look.

- *Higher rise to downplay curves:* If you are curvy and you want to hide your stomach, I recommend going for a high-rise jean, as this will hold everything in.

- *Lower rise to enhance curves:* If you are a slimmer apple shape, then lower-rise jeans can give you a more curvy appearance.

- *Trouser jeans:* If you want to balance things out, I recommend going for a trouser-style jean, as the wider leg from hip to foot will help with proportions.

Jeans for Rectangle and Boy Body Shapes

This is the classic supermodel shape: extra height, long legs, and a straighter hip area. You can find it hard to get jeans to fit in length and be flattering and feminine. But don't worry: There are plenty of choices for you. Look for these:

- *Long inseams:* If you want to go for a smart look, long inseams are the way to go for sleek, clean lines. If you prefer something more fashionable and love the look of jeans with ankle boots, go for a cropped skinny and cuff them with your ankle boots. This will give more

depth to your shape and lessen your height a little bit while looking chic.

- *Skinny jeans:* Skinnies are always your best friend, as they show off your figure beautifully. Just be sure to pick the most flattering pair for your butt and thighs.

- *Skinny flares:* You can also get away with skinny flares, as you have the height to pull it off. Don't do baggy flares, as they will overwhelm you. Make sure the flare starts below the knee.

- *Higher rise to enhance height:* If you want to show off your height, go for a high rise.

- *Lower rise to downplay height:* If you want to make your legs more proportional, a low rise will work wonders.

- *Boyfriend jeans:* You can get away with boyfriend jeans and make them look amazing! Go for a slimmer-fitting boyfriend and it will look great.

Jeans for Square and Athletic Body Shapes

If you have worked hard enough to get an athletic body shape, there are still numerous jeans that can work for you. You don't have to stick to the men's department at all! Look for these options:

- *Stretch denim:* It's important to go with a thicker, stretchier fabric, as rigid denim will not be comfortable on your muscular thighs. Make sure the denim is very stretchy, as you need to keep your thighs slim and the butt tight too. I don't recommend sizing up to accommodate your thighs in stiffer denim, as the butt will end up baggy.

- *Wide leg:* If you are having trouble finding tighter fitting jeans to fit your thighs and butt, try a trouser-style wide-leg jean. They are loose enough to accommodate and will be flattering.

- *Boyfriend jeans:* If a more casual appearance is your thing, then I definitely say boyfriend jeans are the way to go. They are extra

roomy in the butt and the thighs and will be comfortable.

- *Straighter-hip fits:* You want to look for jeans that run larger in the waist than most, as they will help fit smoothly against the square shape of the hips.

- *Higher rise:* If you are carrying a lot of muscle in the butt and hip area, I recommend a higher rise, as you don't want the dreaded builder's or plumber's butt syndrome.

What to Wear . . . Under There: A Guide to What Goes Underneath

No one ever wants to admit they committed a fashion faux pas, but we're going to, for the sake of sharing what we learned. Jené's "crime of fashion" first came to light at a bridal shower and, as an already established bra expert, that's when her love for another underpinning staple—shapewear—began.

Jené was wearing this fabulous Diane von Furstenberg wrap dress with a pair of Michael Kors gladiator sandals. A pretty pulled-together outfit, or so she thought . . . until she noticed an aunt eyeballing her from across the room with what she could easily detect as a look of disapproval. Jené walked over to see what the matter was and her aunt whispered to her, almost as if to tell her a secret, "Honey, you need a slip." Jené thought, *A slip? Why would I need one of those? Who has even worn one of those since the Hindenburg?*

Moments later, Jené's ex-husband's grandmother snuck up behind her, smacked her squarely in the buttocks, and exclaimed, "Sweetie, you need some Spanx!" Spanx? As in shapewear? "Isn't that, like, a *girdle*?" Jené replied. "I don't even *own* those!" Her ex's grandmother retorted, "Well, you should—you have visible panty lines!" In horror, Jené ran to the ladies' room only to discover that, although slight, yes, those panty lines were indeed visible.

The stereotype of shapewear is that it's only to be used when you feel like you're losing the battle of the bulge—you know, go ahead, have that extra doughnut and pour yourself into some Spanx tomorrow; no one will know the difference. But shapewear can do so much more than erase panty lines under nearly any

Shaping Brief   Mid-Thigh Shaper   Shaping Slip

fabric (no matter how clingy). In the years since, Jené has become a huge advocate of shapewear for all shapes and sizes to mask a multitude of bodily sins. Jacqueline is a huge fan as well, which is why we decided to give you some advice based on what we've learned!

If you've tried shapewear, then you know that some of it can make you feel like sausage stuffed into casing. But with the market for shaping garments exploding of late, what's out there is more than just your grandma's girdle. So before someone points out *your* VPL (visible panty lines), we're revealing some of the latest and greatest options in shapewear—and where you can find them.

Types of Shapewear

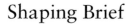

The first step to choosing shapewear is figuring out what you want to "shape." These needs could change depending on the outfit. Are you looking for tummy control? Would you like more waist definition? What about smoothing your torso

(buh-bye, back fat!), rear, or thighs? Pinpointing what you're looking for your shaper to *do* will help you invest in the right pieces (and we say "invest" because shapers aren't cheap).

There are a few different styles to choose from, from a variety of brands, at a variety of price points. Now you can find shapewear at pretty much any mass-market store.

SHAPING PANTIES

We like to think of these as an introductory course to shapewear. These allow you to flatten your tummy and hips while lifting and supporting your rear, but only go up as high as your natural waist. They look kind of like spandex bike shorts and simply smooth hips, rear, and thighs, without a whole lot of other bells and whistles. Once you try a pair of these, you will be sold on shapewear's place in your life. Shapewear also smoothes out the unsightly lumps and bumps of cellulite to give you a more toned appearance in your clothes, especially when worn under thin material!

Light compression	Sort of like control-top panty hose, this sucks you in a bit and smooths you out while still allowing some breathability and comfort.
Moderate compression	A step up from the light-control versions, these shapers often have control panels or other added features.
Firm compression	These control problem areas with heavy construction and control panels.
Extra-firm compression	Typically these include reinforced panels and sometimes even boning for maximum, extra-firm control.

HIGH-WAIST BODY SHAPERS

These pieces smooth the entire midsection, from the tummy on down through the hips, around the back, and in some cases, the thighs. You can find one with a built-in-bra, or a style that allows you to wear your own bra (such as one of our faves—HookedUp Shapewear, which pulls up underneath the back of your bra band and hooks to the straps so it will *not* roll down!). High-waist shapers often come in several styles: a skirt style, a bike short style, or a bodysuit style that snaps at the crotch and does not offer thigh coverage are all options.

Shaper Support

It's important to note that different shapers offer different levels of slimming and support, based on the fabric and the construction. Some will feel constricting, being meant to whittle you down a dress size or two, while others will feel more stretchy and comfortable and are meant simply to smooth you out under clothes. Some women mistakenly think getting shapewear a size smaller than needed will offer them more control, when in actuality, you should stick to your true size, and look for the features called out in the chart above. When you are shopping for shapewear, it will tell you what compression you are getting on the hang tag.

Bras 101

There's undoubtedly one accessory you won't leave the house without: The Bra. Despite the fact that it's meant to go *underneath* your outfit, that little piece of fabric with its many working parts and many synonyms (the "over-the-shoulder boulder holder," the brassiere) can make or break an outfit. And chances are, if you're like an estimated 85 percent of women, you're wearing the wrong one. As the author of *The Bra Book*, Jené has discovered how important this garment is for women of all ages, shapes, sizes, and walks of life. We all seem to come together on this one very important topic—how hard it is to find the right one!

Bra Sizing

While it's essential to get sized up by a professional (you can visit a specialty store, a Victoria's Secret at the mall, or the lingerie section of department stores), it's even more important to understand how the sizing process works.

Your bra size contains two important figures:

▣ An even number that represents the size of your rib cage (and all the way around your back) and corresponds to the band size

▣ A letter that correlates to your cup size in relation to your band size

CORRECT BRA FIT

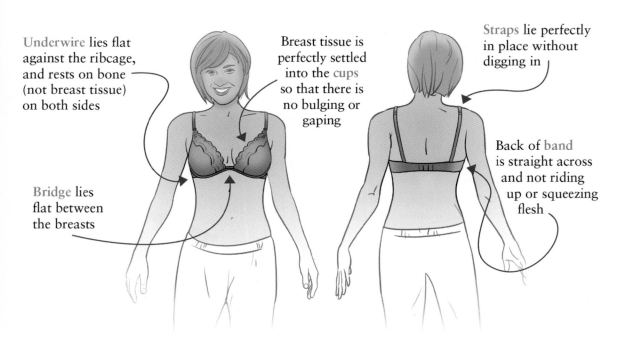

Underwire lies flat against the ribcage, and rests on bone (not breast tissue) on both sides

Breast tissue is perfectly settled into the **cups** so that there is no bulging or gaping

Straps lie perfectly in place without digging in

Bridge lies flat between the breasts

Back of **band** is straight across and not riding up or squeezing flesh

These two figures are proportionate to one another. While it sounds simple, it isn't. There are misconceptions about what these numbers mean in relation to one another. For starters, band size doesn't necessarily equal the width of your rib cage. Often you take the rib cage measurement and will have to add one or two inches to that to get your band size. Also, your band size may vary based on manufacturer and style. A 34 in one style may feel just right, while a 34 in another may be too tight. Your band size is estimated *based* on the width of your rib cage, but it isn't an exact science.

Now, what's also inconsistent is your band size *in relation to* your cup size. For example, an A cup on a 32 band size is not the same as an A cup on the 34 band size, and so on. Instead, the size of, or volume held by, an A cup changes depending on the band size.

What this means in practical terms is that if you go down a band size, you can generally go up in cup size—and vice versa—and achieve a similar fit, because each of these combinations of "sizes" is made to hold the same "volume" of breast tissue. Take this scenario for example: You are in your favorite lingerie store and you spot a bra you absolutely *have* to have. However, you are a 36C and they don't have your size. What to do? You might be able to actually go with the 34D. Just because a D is thought to be larger than a C doesn't mean it actually is. It's just larger than a C in the same band size. The snugger band size actually increases the width and depth of the cup. This is explained in greater detail in *The Bra Book*.

Bra Shopping: How Many and Which Types?

You'll want to have a rotation of at least seven bras. An easy way to remember how many to get is to have one for each day of the week. Get bras in the following types, each starting with an *s*:

- a strapless—or convertible or "multi-way"—bra (versatile styles that will take you from a day at the office to your best friend's wedding with just the switch of the straps)

- a "spa" bra for comfort

- a "specialty" bra (such as a deep plunge, depending on what's in your wardrobe)

- a sports bra

- three "sexy" bras for special occasions or simply for everyday use (who doesn't want to feel sexy under their work suit?)

When bra shopping, also be mindful of the colors you wear most. You can't go wrong with an array of nude and black bras. Now, go get yourself sized up and get shopping!

7 Fashion Cheats to Look Thinner by Dinner

1. Shapewear and back-slimming bras can make you look up to a size smaller—in a snap!

2. Cutouts have been a huge trend the past few seasons and, believe it or not, can actually be a "fashion cheat" to create the illusion of

DIY: Calculating Your Bra Size

Step 1: First, wrap a tape measure (the sewing kind, not the toolbox kind) around your rib cage just below your bust (be sure to exhale first) and take the measurement. Since bra band sizes are even, round up if your measurement is an odd number. For example, if you measure at an odd 31 inches, round up to 32.

Step 2: Next, wrap the tape measure around the fullest part of your bust. Then subtract your band size from this number and use the difference in inches to calculate your cup size. For example, if your bust measurement is an inch larger than your band size, your cup size will most likely be an A; if your bust measurement is two inches larger than your band size, your cup size will most likely be a B; and so on.

Note that sizes vary widely by brand, so this is only meant to be a *guideline*.

3. Most people don't pay much attention to hemlines, but they can really make or break a streamlined silhouette. The key with skirts is that they hit just above the knee, for the longest leg line possible!

4. Who says dressing warm has to mean looking like the Michelin Man? Leggings and layered knits are a classic and comfy look for all women, but sometimes can make you look larger. Simply cinch layers with a skinny belt just below the bustline (at the slimmest part of your torso) to show off your waist, and voilà . . . instant slimming! You can even use a belt over your coat!

5. Pointy pumps with a thinner heel instantly elongate the frame and create a long, lean leg line! Also, a nude or skin-colored pump or even yellow can have that same effect. If choosing platforms, look for a peep-toe style or even a d'Orsay that has lower sides.

6. V- or plunging necklines visually slim the torso. Long necklaces can have the same effect.

7. Go fitted. It's a myth that bigger clothes will make you look smaller. In fact, clothing should be body skimming—not tight and ill fitting!

a smaller waist. If you're not bold enough to try actual cutouts, instead look for dark or mesh panels that instantly draw the eye inward for the appearance of a nipped-in waistline!

Swimming into Style

Sometimes even the smartest women get stumped in the swimwear department. (Trust us, we dread bathing suit shopping too!) According to *Women's Health* magazine, the average woman owns three

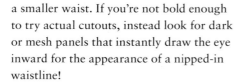

bathing suits, most of which get replaced each year. And any woman will tell you, shopping for them is no day at the beach. In fact, in a survey conducted by *Fitness Magazine*, 18 percent of women would rather go to the dentist—or walk on hot coals—than shop for a swimsuit!

In a recent survey by Lands' End of more than 1,000 women, eight out of ten confessed to wearing the wrong size swimsuit and reported battling unsexy issues like saggy bottoms, cleavage overflow, seat creep, and muffin top. Fifty percent of women have turned down party invitations simply because they required wearing a swimsuit, and 45 percent would never walk around the beach or pool without covering up first.

Instead of just picking whatever's on the rack that fits, or the same old style year after year, try using this guide below to figure out how to accentuate what you've got!

For Itty-Bitty Boobies

It's no secret that swimwear is about showing off some skin—so those who are particularly "less endowed" may be a bit more self-conscious. (But trust us, so are your bigger-boobed counterparts!) If you are part of the itty-bitty-titty committee, look for a bandeau-style top that has some embellishments (ruffles are a fun choice!) or even the new cropped-top styles, or a surfer-girl-esque rash guard. You can also choose a bralike top that has an underwire and some padding so it'll do the same thing your bra does for you!

For Big Boobies

String bikinis are not your best friend (we cringe when we see boob peeking out the bottom!). Look for a bra-sized swimsuit with an underwire and thicker straps for extra support. Julie Joa is a great swimwear line—Jené even designed a collection for her, drawing from her bra expertise. The entire line is based on your bra size, with great support for B cups and up. So, no more panic when you see that S, M, L, and don't quite know where you fit in.

For a Flat Booty

So, we've covered the T . . . can't forget the A. Booties are highlighted just as much as boobies are when it comes to swim attire. And if yours is exactly the opposite of Kim Kardashian's, you may want to give it a little boost. Look for cheeky bottoms with prints and lots of color that offer moderate to minimal coverage.

For a Big Booty

If you are more of the J. Lo/Beyoncé/Kardashian variety but it's not exactly your "moneymaker," you may want to deemphasize this ample asset when you hit the beach. That's where full-coverage bottoms come in. You can choose a two-piece suit that has a print up top with a solid darker color on the bottom, to draw the eye up and away from the rearview. You can also opt for a swim skirt, which will help mask fuller thighs.

For a Straight Body

Want to create a waistline where there isn't one? Choose an of-the-moment one-piece style or a monokini with side cutouts. Opting for one that also has a built-in bra will add some extra curves.

For Tummy Troubles

You can go for a tankini that skims the midsection (but look for a built-in bra so it boosts; no sagging!)

A cropped top can help balance a smaller bust

A tankini can help mask a fuller tummy

A swim skirt is a great way to conceal fuller thighs

Look for bra-sized tops and thicker straps to support a bigger bust

Minimize your bottom half with a solid color bottom and printed top

Higher cut bottoms lengthen the leg

A monokini with side cutouts adds curves to a straight body

or a one-piece with some ruching across the tummy area to whittle the middle! High-waisted retro-style bottoms can also be a fun choice to mask a full tummy or muffin top; just be sure to only show about an inch or two of skin between the bikini top and the top of the bottoms—it should come up above your belly button.

Get Sexy! Shopping for Lingerie

Unlike bras or shapers, lingerie has a less functional purpose. And unlike swimwear, it's about showing skin but not to the general, *ahem*, viewing public. Shopping for lingerie can be an embarrassing notion for many women who are shy about showing off their sexier sides. But once you get past any red-faced moments, you'll discover that dressing up in the bedroom can be just as fun for you as it is for your partner. Oh, and we also promote wearing lingerie all year round, not just on Valentine's Day or anniversaries and other special occasions. It's kinda like saving that fine china for Thanksgiving or Christmas . . . when you could be enjoying dinner on it regularly (wink, wink).

Quick Style Tip

Remember this 'cuz it's simple: Boy-short-style bottoms make your legs look shorter, whereas higher-cut legs (aka French cut) make them look looonger.

Here are our top tips for getting your sexy on. (Your significant other can thank us later!)

1. Either go in with a completely open mind or have an idea of what you're looking for. Lingerie can range from dominatrix-style dress-up (naughty nurse, anyone?) to a sweet and demure silk robe and negligee. Have an idea of what you think you'd be comfortable in before you hit the store. Or, if you're daring to try it all and see what strikes you, go in with a completely open mind—and you may just have a *Fifty Shades of Grey* moment!

2. Think outside the bedroom box. If you typically wear those men's-style PJ sets, go ahead and put one on, but with the sexiest and laciest bra and undies set you can find underneath it. Let him think it's just a regular night in bed, until you start . . . unbuttoning . . . one by one . . . and there's

a sexy surprise underneath that he'll never forget!

3. Garters and thigh-highs. Men love these—they scream sex. Need we say more? If you're unsure how to properly put them on or wear them, ask the salesperson for a tutorial. Add a sexy bra, and voilà, instant sex kitten.

4. Shop for your shape. Lingerie is all about what you *feel* best in. If you feel uncomfortable or unsexy in it, it will show, and that defeats the purpose! Use lingerie to highlight your best assets! For example, if you've shied away from sexy underthings because you've put on a few pounds, shop for pieces that'll accentuate what you've got. We are huge fans of corsets and what they can do for your shape. They're not only sexy without showing a ton of skin, but they boost the bust and whittle the middle and can be multipurpose pieces in that they can be worn both in and out of the bedroom.

5. Don't forget a few key accoutrements. Lots of women think of lingerie when it comes to spicing things up, but there are plenty of fun accessories you can try as well. Don't shy away from trying flavored massage oils or lubricants, paint-on body powders, silk masks, or even handcuffs—the sky's the limit, and sex is supposed to be fun!

When it comes to creating your own personal style, you can get as creative as you want. As long as you feel good and confident when you look in the mirror, you can wear anything your heart desires! Screw what anyone else thinks! You may want to wear one item on trend, or many at once, or maybe you don't want to be trendy at all. That's okay. And don't get too caught up in wishing you had a different body shape and size than the one you've been gifted, because what you have is beautiful too! There is no ideal body type, shape, or size. It's all about embracing and loving what we've got!

Taking Care of Your Delicates

When it comes to caring for fine washables like shapers, bras, lingerie, and swimwear, you want to be mindful of their delicate construction and fabrics. If you must machine wash, use a mesh garment bag, cool water, a gentle detergent, and a gentle cycle if your machine has one. You can also hand wash with plain old baby shampoo!

CHAPTER 10

Now You've GOT IT!

One of the secrets we've learned on our journeys thus far is that you should never stop growing, learning, and evolving, and you should always, *always* be grateful for everything you have in this life. We believe that having an attitude of gratitude just makes even more good things come your way! At any given time, there are always going to be areas in our lives where we will be struggling. The truth is, everyone has room for improvement in their lives. But we have to hope, believe, trust, and pray that everything will happen for the greater good. Be open to change, look for the positive and the lesson in all things, and accept the things you can't change or control!

In this book, we've provided you with practical tips to maximize your time and take care of yourself—inside *and* out. We hope you've learned a few things you can take with you as you continue on your journey in life, whether you're a mom, wife, career woman, lover, or friend.

Remember that beauty is not about flawless makeup or never having a hair out of place—it's about being the healthiest you can be and feeling your best from the inside out, giving you self-confidence and positive energy that projects onto others. Make a promise to yourself that self-care will always be a priority, and commit to doing more of the things that bring you happiness. Here's a list of some of *our* favorite gateways to peace and fulfillment:

- Get enough rest! It allows you to recharge, regroup, and reconnect with yourself and stay healthy overall. Never skimp on sleep!

- Say positive affirmations daily! Look at yourself in the mirror each day and list all the things you like about yourself, as well as how you envision your life to be. A little positivity goes a long way!

- Set goals and make to-do lists, and look at your vision board daily! Create a vision and a detailed plan for achieving it, with both short- and long-term goals. Check off your accomplishments as you go through your daily to-do lists.

- Squeeze in some exercise daily! Be it a nature walk, thirty minutes of yoga on your living room floor, or a few reps of arm curls at your desk, working your body will also work wonders for your mind and soul.

- Eat well and never skip a meal! A splurge or cheat day here and there is not a bad thing, but in general, try to eat a healthy, balanced diet, drink plenty of water, and definitely don't skip meals. Breakfast like a king, lunch like a queen, and dinner like a pauper will keep your body properly fueled and running efficiently all the time.

- Learn to effectively manage your feelings and emotions! Whether through exercise, meditation, or simply taking ten deep breaths, figure out ways to nip stress, anxiety, frustration, and anger in the bud before they wreak havoc on your body. Left unchecked, they can cause myriad health problems.

- Tackle a bad habit! Whether it's too much alcohol, a fast-food addiction, or smoking, do your best to kick your worst habit (and not just around the New Year!). And don't do it for anyone else but yourself! It takes about twenty-one days to break a habit, and if you focus on making small positive changes every single day, then one day at a time, your life will change for the better.

- Complete at least one organizational task daily! Cross something off your to-do list every day: Organize a drawer, clean out one shelf in your refrigerator, do a load of laundry, tidy up your desk. Whatever it is, quit procrastinating and just do it!

- Do something you're passionate about! Nothing brings you more joy than spending time doing something that activates your passion. Whatever it is, make it your hobby or make it your career, as long as you're making time to do it.

- Spread kindness! Whether it's holding the door open for the person behind you, letting someone in front of you in the grocery line, or even just smiling at a stranger, try to spread kindness like confetti. What you put out will come back to you—we promise!

- Communicate your feelings to others! It's important to say what's on your mind, but remember, delivery is everything. Use discretion if it's something that will be hurtful to the other person and will have no benefit to either of you. But that said, it's easy to fall into a trap where we hold in our thoughts and feelings for fear of hurting someone else's. Your feelings matter too, so keep the lines of communication open with the loved ones in your life!

- Self-reflect! Try to understand what lessons you've learned from your past experiences, and then think about how you will apply those lessons going forward.

- Forgive someone! Let go of the anger, bitterness, and resentment you feel toward others and allow yourself to see things from someone else's perspective. Accept that you can't control others' actions—only your reactions to their actions. Remember that you can't change people, but you can appreciate them for who they are.

- ▣ **Make a donation to charity and/or volunteer!** If you're able to donate some time, some cash, or some food or used clothes, giving to those in need not only makes someone else feel good, but can make you feel good as well.

- ▣ **Engage in daily prayer or meditation!** Ten minutes of asking a higher power for guidance and clarity can work wonders for releasing stress, worry, guilt, and/or self-doubt.

- ▣ **Be grateful!** Always count your blessings at the end of the day. Realizing all that you have to be grateful for and all that's positive in your life can bring you joy and add an instant smile to your face.

Quit waiting around or depending on others to bring you peace and happiness. Go out there and *get it* yourself!! You don't need someone else to take you to the movies, buy you flowers, or help you enjoy your favorite activity. Treat yourself! Do the things that bring you joy and make you smile, even if it's just for a moment. Remember: Your happiness comes from your own perception. So choose to be happy by perceiving the world around you as a beautiful and positive place. There is beauty in everything if you just look past the negative and seek out the positive. Doing this will invite more positivity in your life. Seek positivity and you will find positivity; seek negativity and you will find negativity.

We suggest you take a few minutes to make a Happy List of all the things, large and small, that bring you joy. These are all things that make great "me time" activities! Here's a sampling of our Happy List to help you get started:

- ▣ Sitting outside having a cup of coffee or tea and enjoying nature

- ▣ A bubble bath with candlelight, soft music, and a glass of bubbly or cup of hot chamomile tea

- ▣ Going for a walk, run, or hike outdoors

- ▣ Watching a favorite old "feel good" movie

- ▣ Getting a manicure, pedicure, or massage

- ▣ Catching up with friends

- ▣ Reading in a favorite spot

- ▣ Surfing the internet, discovering new videos on YouTube, or catching up with friends on social media

- ▣ Sitting on a beach, watching the waves

"Happiness is being at peace with what is. It is trusting what your past was, your present is, and your future will be."

—Donna M. Thomas

- Journaling

- Volunteer work

- Retail therapy (as long as you don't overspend!)

- Meditating

- Doing a homemade hair or skin mask

- Listening to motivational CDs or podcasts

- Trying out a new recipe

- Visiting a park, zoo, or museum

- Making a vision board

- Sending ourselves flowers, or going somewhere we can pick them up

- Taking a road trip and/or exploring somewhere new

Make your own Happy List, and then be sure to look at it often and make time to do those things more regularly! Learn how to slow down, be grateful for what you have and where you've been, and just enjoy the moment you're in. There's a lot to be said for living in the present!

Life is full of up and downs, and we will always be faced with challenges. No matter how bad things may seem at certain times in your life, know that you will get through it. Remember, too, that every flower has to grow through dirt; life's tough times and challenges will only make you stronger in the end.

Find your best way around those obstacles and use the lessons learned along the way. Share your knowledge with others. Keep your chin up and keep moving forward and upward. The cream always rises to the top, ladies!

Believe that you are a beautiful, strong, powerful, confident, successful woman and keep striving to be the best you can be, every single day. Now you *get it*!

ACKNOWLEDGMENTS

I want to thank my loving family—my husband Chris, my daughter Ashlee, and my two sons CJ and Nicholas—for their patience, love, and support while I researched and wrote this book, and for the way they always encourage me to share my passion with others! I want to thank my little brother Tom and my sister-in-law Mary for their feedback and help in condensing my ramblings to a smaller word count during their vacation.

I also want to thank the professionals who shared their knowledge with Jené and me, in order to pass that knowledge on to you: Samanta Bianco, Lorna Burford, Dr. Ramtin Kassir, Jolene Matthews, George Miguel, and Dr. William Song.

Thank you to our publisher Glenn for giving us this opportunity, and to the amazing team at BenBella who worked so hard for us and had faith in us that we would complete this book—even when we were taking forever!

Last but not least, a huge thank you to my friend and coauthor Jené Luciani for coming up with the brilliant idea for us to join forces and expertise in order to create this guide to help busy girls like ourselves live a more positive and fulfilling life amid the chaos—and look great while doing it. Life is good!

—*Jacqueline*

I'd like to first and foremost acknowledge my wonderful coauthor Jacqueline Laurita, who is SO talented, SO caring, SO smart, and has SO many other qualities I admire that there isn't even enough time to show them on reality TV!

Thank you to my family: my boyfriend Patrick and our children GiGi, Ayva, Patrick, and Kalen, who constantly bring smiles and make all the hard work worthwhile; my parents Rose and Lyle and Tony and Michele; Jess and Frank and Jarid and Felicia; and the rest of my family and friends for their continued support. (Mom, I can always count on you to visit Barnes & Noble and make sure they move my books to a higher shelf—haha!)

Also Glenn, Adrienne, Leah, Heather, Sarah, and the entire team at BenBella Books, as well as my literary agent Michael Ebeling—thank you for always believing in me and my vision! We all have a lifelong friendship and partnership that I know is rare and special in the publishing industry, and I am so grateful for it.

And of course, thank you to my talent agent, Mark Turner at Abrams Artists Agency, and all of the producers I work with continuously for various media outlets (especially the *TODAY* show gang) that like me enough to put me on their shows!

Plus a special thanks to all the women out there doing the daily hustle and making it happen. This is for all of you. *Get it*, ladies!

—Jené

ABOUT THE AUTHORS

Best known for her roles as an original cast member on Bravo's *The Real Housewives of New Jersey* and on the new Bravo series *Manzo'd with Children*, **Jacqueline Laurita** is a well-known TV personality, mom, wife, philanthropist, and businesswoman.

While millions follow her life on TV and on social media, Laurita is also a twenty-year beauty industry veteran: a licensed cosmetologist with a passion for all things beauty, including hair, makeup, and skin care. Aside from her work in front of and behind the camera, Laurita has tested and consulted for a number of power players in the cosmetics industry. She will continue to share her passion with others on her beauty, wellness, and lifestyle blog, *The LookOver*, which will be featured on JacquelineLaurita.com.

An avid philanthropist, Jacqueline is a celebrity ambassador to several nonprofit autism organizations. Her mission is not only to help her youngest son, Nicholas, reach his fullest potential, but also to assist other families facing the same diagnosis. She regularly travels the country as a sought-after public speaker raising autism awareness, including giving

keynote speeches alongside her husband Chris at conferences, colleges, and fundraising benefits. Jacqueline and Chris will share their struggles and successes raising a child with special needs, while coping with difficult times as a family and keeping a strong and healthy marriage, in their forthcoming book *Defy Expectations* (BenBella Books).

Jacqueline and Chris live in New Jersey with their children, Ashlee, CJ, and Nick, and their Cavalier King Charles Spaniel, Santino.

Hailed as a "brilliant bra guru" by BRAVO-TV, "the country's foremost authority on all things bras" by Dr. Oz, and a "stylist extraordinaire" and "bra fit guru" by the *New York Daily News* and *Woman's World Magazine*, **Jené Luciani** is a nationally acclaimed fashion journalist, lifestyle expert, tastemaker, TV personality, spokesperson, and author. She hosted Lifetime Network's *Mom's Personal Shopper* series on the Lifetime Moms channel, and she appears regularly on NBC's *TODAY*, *The Wendy Williams Show*, *Dr. Oz*, and *The Meredith Vieira Show*, among others. She has hundreds of published bylines to her name in publications such as *SHAPE* and the *Huffington Post*, and is the author of the bestselling *The Bra Book: The Fashion Formula to Finding the Perfect Bra* (BenBella Books, 2009), with a revised and expanded second edition due out in 2017.

When she's not appearing on TV or giving advice in print, Jené is a busy mom in sweats leading a "quiet life" in upstate New York with her boyfriend and children, while also enjoying serving as mistress-of-ceremonies for and on the committees of numerous philanthropic causes. You can find out more about her by visiting her website at JeneLuciani.com.

PHOTO AND IMAGE CREDITS

Box illustrations throughout the text and illustration on page 160 by Ralph Voltz.

Photos on pages xiv, 20, 32, 50, 80, 100, 120, and 148 by Matt Hoyle; makeup by Heather Adessa and hair by Kristina Pettignano of Glo Beauty Bar; styling by Nathan Helsel of Out of The Box Style.

Photos on pages xiv and 20, clothing courtesy of T.J.Maxx.

Photos on pages 10 and 100, clothing courtesy of Marshalls.

Photo on page 32, clothing courtesy of Calvin Klein and Akira.

Photo on page 120, clothing courtesy of Tees by Tina.

Photo on page 148, clothing courtesy of Adrianna Papell and Akira.

Photo on page 5 © pab_map/Fotolia.

Photo on page 6 © Rostislav Sedlacek/Fotolia.

Right-hand photo on page 10 by T.R. Laz.

Photo on page 11 © Aleksandar Mijatovic/Fotolia.

Photo on page 25 © iStock.com/grafvision.

Photo on page 27 © osorioartist/Fotolia.

Photo on page 28 © Marco Desscouleurs/Fotolia.

Photo on page 30 © iStock.com/KatarzynaBialasiewicz.

Photo on page 34 © iStock.com/aluxum.

Photo on page 36 © iStock.com/aluxum.

Photos on pages 59–78 by Manny Carabel–MTC Photography.

Photo on page 66 © iStock.com/Steve Debenport.

Photo on page 82 © ag visuell/Fotolia.

Photo on page 92 © milanmarkovic78/Fotolia.

Photos on pages 95–98 © 3xy/Fotolia.

Photo on page 102 © iStock.com/ttsz.
Photo on page 117 © Africa Studio/Fotolia.
Photo on page 119 © iStock.com/wragg.
Photo on page 122 © millefloreimages/Fotolia.

Photo on page 130 © picsfive/Fotolia.
Photo on page 133 © imagehub/Fotolia.

Photo on page 143 © imagehub/Fotolia.
Photo on page 154 © Cherries/Fotolia.

Photos on page 153 courtesy of . . .
  Fashions by Catherines®/www.catherines.com
    (3, 6, 7, 11, 12).
  HookedUp Shapewear/www.
    hookedupshapewear
    .com (2), all rights reserved.
  Lands' End/www.landsend.com (9, 13, 17, 19).

Fotolia (1 [©Gordana Sermek/Fotolia], 4
  [©Tarzhanova/Fotolia], 5 [©stringerphoto
  /Fotolia], 8 [©srki66/Fotolia], 10 [©photo
  -nuke/Fotolia], 14 [©Tarzhanova/Fotolia], 16
  [©Michael Flippo/Fotolia]).
iStockPhoto (15 [©iStockPhoto/NAKphotos],
  18 [©iStockPhoto/Omer Yurdakul
  Gundogdu]).

Photos on page 158 courtesy of Hooked Up
  Shapewear (www.hookedupshapewear.com),
  all rights reserved.
Photos on page 164 provided by Joa Swim LLC
  (www.juliejoa.com).
Photo on page 165 © iStock.com/RichHobson.

Photo on page 173 by Giulianna Marie and Flo.
Photo on page 174 by Emily Valentine.

THE BRA BOOK

The Fashion Formula to Finding the Perfect Bra

The Bra Book author Jené Luciani—a fashion expert and a go-to guide for beauty advice—once and for all arms women with the knowledge they need to find the right fashion support. From the best bra to wear under every outfit to important information about bras and breast health from puberty to retirement, from the physics behind bra design to how you can best ensure a proper fit, *The Bra Book* is the source for women everywhere.

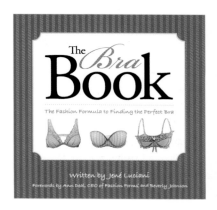

Jené Luciani is a nationally acclaimed fashion journalist, lifestyle expert, tastemaker, TV personality, spokesperson, and author. When she's not appearing on TV or giving advice in print, she's leading a "quiet life" in upstate New York with her boyfriend and children.

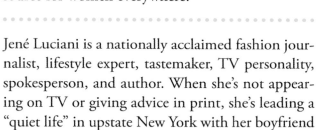

Visit JeneLuciani.com
to learn more!